cookies

for kids' cancer

ALL THE GOOD COOKIES

Gretchen Holt-Witt

with Fraya Berg and Jackie Plant

Photography by Lucy Schaeffer

cookies
for kids' cancer

❀

ALL THE GOOD COOKIES

HMH
HOUGHTON MIFFLIN HARCOURT
Boston   New York
2013

Photography copyright © 2013 by Lucy Schaeffer

Food styling by Cyd McDowell

Prop styling by Michelle Rotman Jassem

Cover image: Lucy Schaeffer

Cover design: Suzanne Sunwoo

Interior design by Cassandra J. Pappas

Published by Houghton Mifflin Harcourt Publishing
Company, New York, New York

For information about permission to reproduce selections
from this book, write to Permissions, Houghton Mifflin Harcourt Publishing Company, 215 Park Avenue South, New York,
New York, 10003.

www.hmhbooks.com

Library of Congress Cataloging-in-Publication Data
Holt-Witt, Gretchen, 1967-
   Cookies for kids' cancer: just the cookies / Gretchen Holt-
Witt; with Fraya Berg and Jackie Plant; photography by Lucy
Schaeffer.
      p. cm.
   Includes index.
ISBN 978-1-118-32952-8 (cloth); ISBN 978-1-118-45684-2 (ebk);
ISBN 978-1-118-45685-9 (ebk); ISBN 978-1-118-45686-6 (ebk)
   1. Cookies. 2. Cancer in children—Psychological aspects.
I. Berg, Fraya. II. Plant, Jackie. III. Title.
   TX772.W5486 2013
   641.86'54—dc23   2012023279

Printed in China
10 9 8 7 6 5 4 3 2 1

To Liam

Our sweet pumpkin and master chef
who taught us how to live, love, and laugh.
We miss you in everything we do,
but everything we do is to honor you.
Love,
Mommy, Daddy, and Ella

"The first time his laughter unfurled its wings
in the wind, we knew that the world
would never be the same."
—Brian Andreas

contents

foreword

Many of us have experienced or will experience the "bad thing" at some point in life. The needle scratches across the record with the news; forward movement stops with the phone call, the diagnosis. It is particularly painful when the bad thing happens to a child. And yet, while Gretchen and her family were battling back stage 4 cancer with their beloved son, she chose to do an extraordinary thing. Watching Liam's journey and that of the other families on the cancer ward, Gretchen decided to do what she could to ensure that others would not have to walk that same devastating path. She organized an army of devoted friends and admirers to mix, bake, package, and distribute thousands of cookies that offered a sweet promise for finding a cure.

I met Gretchen more than twenty years ago in Richmond, Virginia. In those early years I don't think either of us could have imagined what life had in store for us, good and bad. We each had one another's back as I nursed my husband through his critical wounds during the Iraq war and then just a year later she got the devastating news about Liam. I can still remember exactly where I was standing and how the sunlight knifed across my kitchen floor when she called to tell me.

Liam was a beloved little boy. And he loved life right back. He was an old soul, wise and patient and thoughtful. But he was also like a vacuum cleaner, sucking up all there was to learn, know, enjoy, and share in the world. And when he became ill, Gretchen's job was to shelter him from the reality of his disease so that he could live his life to the fullest. It is a testament to them both that Liam never knew he had cancer. Despite the pain and discomfort he suffered at times, Liam looked forward to the things that made him happy: scootering on the New York sidewalks, playing with his adoring sister Ella, watching every cooking show he could find, and visiting the local fire station. Cookies for Kids' Cancer was an extension of the weekend hobby he loved: baking. For Liam, baking, being together, and Cookies were all one big way to help other kids and to share his love.

This book is not only a wonderful collection of yummy recipes, but a road map that outlines how you can do something to help, right in your own kitchen. Holding a bake sale in your neighborhood, school, or community brings us all one step closer to funding a cure. Anyone can get involved in Cookies, at any age, to help make a difference in the lives of children, to protect those we love most, and to give a voice to those who don't have one. In the end, that's really what Cookies is all about—an act of love and kindness.

—LEE WOODRUFF, author of *Those We Love Most*

preface

As food editors in the early '90s, we met Gretchen when she came by our test kitchens to introduce us to the newest kitchen gadgets. When we became the best of friends, we discovered that Gretchen was just one more thing we had in common. In 2007, we were working together as the food editors at *Parents* creating recipes for families when we got the news that Liam had cancer. It's hard to explain how, during the course of reading an email, time stops and moves into warp speed simultaneously. Our focus was helping Gretchen and her family in any way we could, which at that time became a mix of cooking food to bring to the hospital, showering Liam's sister Ella with oodles of attention, and baking, baking, baking. Every trip to the hospital began with a package of cookies for the staff labeled "Baked for you with love from the friends of Liam." We, along with a few other amazing women, became "the aunties," women Gretchen knew she could call on with any request. We held hands through surgeries, procedures, clinical trials, and chemo— all of it. Friends and family would ask, "How can you go there, how can you handle being on the pediatric cancer floor?" Our answer was always the same: "How can we not?" So when the request for cookie help

came, there we were, in the trenches with the original 96,000 cookies.

Fast-forward to today. When Gretchen mentioned this book was in the making, we jumped on the idea of contributing to it, actually begging her to let us create the recipes in these pages. With 168 sticks of butter, 62 pounds of flour, 43 pounds of sugar, 19 dozen eggs, vats of chocolate, heaping bowls of nuts, and just enough vanilla and spice to make each recipe delicious and unique, we've baked 320 dozen cookies.

Every cookie in this book also has a secret ingredient: LOVE. It's obvious to us when we are at Cookies for Kids' Cancer bake sales that it's everyone else's secret ingredient too. We know you're going to love these cookies, and we're certain when you bake them you too will be making them with love.

—JACKIE and FRAYA

Jackie Fraya

introduction

In everyone's life, at some time, our inner fire goes out. It is then burst into flame by an encounter with another human being. We should all be thankful for those people who rekindle the inner spirit. —ALBERT SCHWEITZER

I f these pages could talk, if they could literally include my voice, or if I could personally jump through them into your kitchen, cup of coffee in hand, thumbing the pages to pick the perfect recipes for an upcoming Cookies for Kids' Cancer bake sale, we wouldn't just be talking about sweets . . . we would also be talking about change. Because in almost every way, everything in my life has changed since I wrote the introduction of our first Cookies for Kids' Cancer cookbook.

Certainly, there has been good change. Since 2010 when I was working on that manuscript, Cookies for Kids' Cancer as an organization has simply exploded. Every single year, the support for Cookies has doubled. We see the dream we had being realized: to create an easy way for people anywhere, of any age to get involved in pediatric cancer research. With a very small but very passionate team of people led by the indomitable Emily Fowler, who joined as a volunteer and then became our first employee, we see a difference being made in real time. In a million years, I never thought we would actually see the progress of science happening. For the first year or so bake sales were the name of the game, but now they're just one way to "Be a Good Cookie." People are inspired to run 5Ks and marathons, host pancake breakfasts and penny drives—and, of course, there are still bake sales

Mattawan, MI

from desk-side to city-wide happening consistently. And most importantly, because of this growth Cookies for Kids' Cancer has been able to grant millions to pediatric cancer research.

But sadly—tragically—heartbreakingly, the change isn't all good. When the manuscript for our first cookbook was delivered, Liam was 3½ years into his battle with cancer and was spending the hot days of the summer swimming for hours and hours in the pool with his

Los Angeles, CA

beloved sister and best friend Ella. He was sun-kissed and happy, loving every moment of the warm weather. He was in the midst of climbing back from a relapse that spring, but all seemed right in the world. Then, in the weeks after turning in the manuscript to our ever-supportive editor, Justin Schwartz, things changed. Mo-

Arlington, TX

ments of fear turned into days and months of an endless battle against this cruel, cowardly, and unrelenting disease, with the ever-present focus on hope for Liam's health. But for Liam, the happy ending we wanted was not to be. On January 24, 2011, our sweet son's battle with pediatric cancer came to an end after four very long and very hard years. He was 6 years, 8 months, and 9 days old and ready to take on the world.

In the first days and weeks after we said good-bye to Liam, in the midst of unspeakable grief, one truth in my life became clear—even though I could not change the outcome for Liam, the battle wasn't over. Suddenly, we weren't fighting for Liam, we were fighting in honor of Liam and of all kids battling cancer today and

Long Beach, NY

tomorrow. The battle clearly changed, but the mission remained the same. While Liam was completely one of a kind, in terms of the world of pediatric cancer, our sweet pumpkin's story is far too common. Pediatric cancer remains the number one disease killer of children in the United States. It kills more children than asthma, AIDS, multiple sclerosis, and muscular dystrophy . . . combined. It knows no race, creed, religion, or socioeconomic or geographic boundary. It attacks indiscriminately and with no reason other than a bad shuffle in the deck of life. Yet all types of pediatric cancers collectively receive less than 4 percent of the National Cancer Institute's multibillion-dollar budget and an equally appallingly small amount of research dollars from pharmaceutical companies. It's simply not on the radar screen of our government, private industry, or the general public—unless you're personally connected to it.

Prior to Liam's diagnosis, my husband Larry and I would have never set out to launch a national nonprofit organization. But after Liam's first few months of treatment, when he was declared to have "no evidence

Linden, NJ

of disease," we did set out to fight pediatric cancer on the fund-raising front because it was, quite simply, the right thing to do. It all started with the seemingly simple idea to bake a few cookies . . . 96,000 of them, to be exact. It seemed like a reasonable number because after battling cancer, anything seemed reasonable. With an army of 250 volunteers (some of whom knew each other, more of whom did not but who instantly became committed to a cause), we held one giant holiday cookie sale, raised over $420,000, and used every dollar raised to fund a new pediatric cancer

West Seneca, NY

Charlotte, NC

cer treatment in development. But even before the ovens had had the chance to cool, we realized that maybe those cookies could fill a void in the world of pediatric cancer, by adding a sweet spot in an otherwise all-too-often bitter and devastating topic. Typically, it's left up to the mommies and daddies with children battling pediatric cancer to also raise funds to support new therapies for the disease. But with Cookies for Kids' Cancer, our goal is to inspire change by giving people everywhere ideas on how to come forward as Good Cookies and raise funds in an all-out fight against this demon.

And we are making a difference. Already, Cookies for Kids' Cancer has helped jump-start dozens of new research projects. By the time

Amagansett, NY

this book comes out, another round of grants will have been awarded. As one of Liam's oncologists said to me, "It's not science that's holding us back, it's funding." The first project those 96,000 cookies helped fund is now a treatment children are receiving. Other projects will soon move from the lab to the clinic. And one of the grants awarded in 2011 was to a project named by *Discover* magazine as #10 on the Top 100 Scientific Stories of the Year. Together we can make and are making a difference in the battle against pediatric cancer.

But for today, it's really all about the cookies in this book. And my belief is that with these recipes the difference we're making is only the beginning. I truly believe in the magic of cookies and the magic of this book. I hope it brings the same magic to your kitchen that Liam always brought to ours. He loved to bake, and outfitted in an apron and baker's hat, he loved every step of the process, from standing over the mixing bowl to decorating his finished cookies and cakes. He would have loved this book.

It's impossible to look at the recipes and not be inspired to fire up the oven. Each recipe was developed by friends of our family who just happen to be professional chefs and who stepped up to share their love of Cookies for this book. In addition to developing most of the recipes, our dear friends Fraya and Jackie tested and retested every recipe for this book. "Aunt" Fraya and "Aunt" Jackie, as they are known in our home, are so much more than amazing bakers—they were Liam's friends and caregivers to our family through every step of this journey. And they want these cookies to create magic for pediatric cancer research.

And the pictures—have you seen the pictures of the cookies yet? Just thumbing through the book makes me drool, but it also makes my heart burst with joy and love and gratitude for the incomparable Lucy Schaeffer, who lovingly and diligently spent a week finding the perfect light for each picture to make the cookies look simply irresistible.

Edwardsville, IL

And you can't miss the plates, napkins, tags, and bows in the pictures, the handiwork of my dear friend and knock-your-socks-off stylist Michelle Rotman Jassem, who once again offered up her home for a week to serve as our photo studio. It was from the heart that she selected every color and every prop to

Palos Verdes Estates, CA

Boonton Township, NJ

make sure the cookies were the stars of the show. You'll notice more than a few references to the color orange. Liam's love of orange came early and his passion for the color never wavered or waned. He loved its happy disposition and bold statement.

When it comes to food styling, there is nothing like watching an artist at work. Cyd McDowell is one you want to just sit and watch as she creates mouthwatering treats. And Sarah Abrams, who stood by my side baking thousands of cookies back in the early bake-a-thon days, was standing by Cyd's side making sure everything was picture-perfect.

Santa Monica, CA

This book has both heart and soul. The heart can be found in the stories and pictures shared from just a handful of the thousands of events held across the United States and in a baker's dozen of countries around the world. If we had our way, we would have shared the story of every event. But time and space dictated we select a sampling from Good Cookies of all ages who have found a way to get involved and make a difference in the lives of children. Use their words to inspire you. I know they have inspired me to keep moving forward with determi-

New York, NY

nation knowing that change is coming, one Good Cookie at a time.

As our family moves forward, there is continued hope for every child battling cancer. One of Liam's favorite sayings was, "If not NOW, when?" In honor of Liam and in honor of every child—the ones battling cancer today and the ones who will be battling cancer tomorrow—let's be a part of the change NOW. Thank you for your support.

Maplewood, NJ

Package your treats in boxes with peek-a-boo windows. Customers like to see what they are getting.

Stencil a letter or design on a coffee bag to get a super-professional look.

Chinese food containers come in a host of colors and designs. Buy a bunch of them and let your customers package their own treats.

A hole puncher, a length of ribbon, and a name tag are all it takes to make a paper sandwich bag look simply irresistible.

Easy and pretty packaging tips from Michelle Rotman Jassem.

the classic gotta-haves
for a bake sale

rainbow sables

yield: about 7 dozen cookies

A French bakery classic, sables are the epitome of three basic ingredients (butter, sugar, and flour) coming together with little else to create a melt-in-your-mouth delight. Dressed up in sparkling crystal sugar, they shine.

2¼ cups all-purpose flour

⅔ cup granulated sugar

¼ teaspoon salt

2 sticks (½ pound) unsalted butter, cold, cut into 1-inch pieces

1 large egg, at room temperature

1 teaspoon vanilla extract

Colored decorating sugars

- Place the flour, sugar, and salt in the bowl of a food processor fitted with the metal blade. Pulse to combine. Add the butter and pulse to blend until mixture looks like coarse cornmeal. Transfer the mixture to a mixer bowl and add the egg and vanilla. Beat to blend, then scrape down the sides of the bowl and mix again.
- Divide the dough into 5 equal pieces. Form each piece into a 4-inch log and then roll each in a different color of decorating sugar. Cover each log and refrigerate for at least 6 hours and up to 3 days.
- Preheat the oven to 350°F. Line 2 cookie sheets with parchment paper.
- With a serrated knife, cut the logs into ¼-inch slices. Place 1 inch apart on the prepared cookie sheets and bake for 15 to 20 minutes, until the bottoms are lightly browned, rotating the cookie sheets on the oven racks halfway through the baking time. Cool on the cookie sheets for 3 minutes. Transfer to wire racks to cool completely. Repeat with the remaining dough on cool cookie sheets.
- Store in an airtight container for up to 3 days, or freeze for up to 3 months.

sally's potato chip sandies

yield: 6 dozen cookies

Sally, Fraya's mom, has been making these cookies for decades and raving about them. Fraya just couldn't wrap her head around the idea of potato chips in cookies and pooh-poohed them for years until she finally gave in and made them. We now know what all the fuss was about: The butter, nuts, and chips make them short and sweet—and prove that Mom really does know best.

2 sticks (½ pound) unsalted butter, at room temperature

1 cup confectioners' sugar, plus more for dusting (optional)

1 large egg yolk, at room temperature

1 teaspoon vanilla extract

1½ cups all-purpose flour

¾ cup (2½ ounces) crushed potato chips

½ cup finely chopped pecans

- Preheat the oven to 350°F. Line 2 cookie sheets with parchment paper.
- Place the butter and sugar in a large mixer bowl and beat until smooth and creamy, about 3 minutes. Add the egg yolk and vanilla and beat well. With the mixer on low, gradually add flour. Scrape down the sides of the bowl, then gently fold the potato chips and nuts into the dough with a spatula.
- Using a small (2-teaspoon size) cookie scoop, drop scoops of the dough about 2 inches apart on the prepared cookie sheets.
- Transfer to the oven and bake until the cookies begin to brown at the edges, 12 to 15 minutes, rotating the cookie sheets on the oven racks halfway through the baking time. Cool on the cookie sheets for 3 minutes. Transfer to wire racks to cool completely. Repeat with the remaining dough on cool cookie sheets.
- Store in an airtight container for up to 3 days, or freeze for up to 3 months.

mary hickey's toffee bars

yield: 64 bars

Mary Hickey adapted these bars from *The Silver Palate Cookbook* when she was a senior editor at *Parents* magazine, and everyone at her office fell in love with them. She and Sally Lee, *Parents'* editor in chief at the time, secured their spots as true heroes by publishing "A Day in the Life of Liam: Pediatric Cancer Patient," a photo essay, when it seemed no one else wanted to talk about pediatric cancer.

2 sticks (½ pound) unsalted butter, at room temperature

1 cup light brown sugar

⅛ teaspoon salt

1 large egg yolk

1½ teaspoons vanilla extract

2 cups all-purpose flour

2 cups (12 ounces) semi-sweet chocolate chips

1¼ cups coarsely chopped pecans

- Preheat the oven to 350°F. Line a 9 x 13-inch baking pan with foil.

- Place the butter, sugar, and salt in a mixer bowl and beat until smooth and creamy, about 3 minutes. Add the egg yolk and vanilla and beat to combine. With the mixer on low, add the flour and mix to blend well. Scrape down the sides of the bowl and mix again. Press the dough into the bottom of the prepared pan. Transfer to the oven and bake until set and the edges are golden, 25 to 30 minutes.

- Remove the pan from the oven, cover the crust layer with the chocolate chips, and return to the oven for 4 minutes. Remove the pan from the oven and spread the melted chocolate evenly with a spatula. Sprinkle with the nuts. Cool in the pan on a wire rack. When cool, remove from the pan and cut in 64 pieces.

- Store in an airtight container for up to 3 days, or freeze for up to 3 months.

Oyster Bay, NY

ANTONIA WOODMAN
Oyster Bay, NY

- -

Last year, a holiday tradition turned into a student service project when our school's 7th graders heard the story of Liam Witt's courageous battle with cancer and his parents' hope to make a difference for all kids by starting Cookies for Kids' Cancer. The tradition: making gingerbread houses. The service project: selling them as a fundraiser for pediatric cancer research.

Gingerbread houses made by the 7th graders have been a tradition in our school system for over 25 years. The 7th-grade class donated candies and supplies along with two busy weeks of house designing, dough making, cutting, and baking, decorating, and finally selling of the cookie houses.

On the evening of the Winter concert, the 7th graders decorated the auditorium lobby with their gingerbread creations with one new addition—price tags! Oyster Bay residents and school parents came out to attend the concert and had the opportunity to purchase the cookie houses by simply writing a check to Cookies for Kids' Cancer. In one evening with just a few dozen gingerbread houses, we raised $725 for pediatric cancer research. And now, the 7th-grade class can't wait to do it again.

SHARYN BERNARD MULQUEEN
Atlanta, GA

- -

As a longtime supporter, I have held numerous bake sales, but truth be told, I'm not much of a baker and wanted to do something a bit different. At first I wanted to have a big party fundraiser—I even had a venue that was donated, a good deal on a caterer, and was amassing some awesome silent auction items. But one thing and another kept getting in the way, including the fact that ticket sales, at $50 each, were slow and much of that money would be going to the party expense. So I decided to scrap that idea and return to doing what I do best (if I do say so myself): throw a big party at my home! As I say, "When life hands you lemons, grab the vodka."

I had just completed a major kitchen renovation, my family was planning a visit (including my sister who lives in Italy), and it was my birthday, so the timing was perfect. I created a festive e-vite (orange, of course) and a personal giving page requesting donations in lieu of gifts. I also let my friends know that I would hold the silent auction at the party. (I also got a free Square gadget/app for taking payments via credit card—highly recommended.)

I did most of the cooking myself and had a full bar; I also pre-made cosmopolitans and special "Liamtinis"—an orange (and apparently very potent) martini. I hired two college gals to bartend and clean a bit—best decision ever! Friends and I made desserts from the cookbook, as well as the very, very addictive sweet/spicy pecans. I displayed the book and sign cards describing each cookie, and I bought ten books and had them available for "donation" purchase. (I just bought them on Amazon as my donation and sold all of them for $20 each; I easily could have sold more.)

The party was a smash, and I don't just mean because of the drinks! Between the silent auction, my personal giving page, and the cookbook sales, we raised $2,900. I was so happy to do this for my birthday—my friends know how much the Witts and this organization mean to me and were very happy to help and donate.

Carefree, AZ

SHANA BATTLES
Carefree, AZ

We were thrilled to host our first event at the 4th Annual Carefree Christmas Festival in Carefree, Arizona. The festival is a 3-day event that attracts over 20,000 visitors. Our bake sale was one day—Saturday—when over 12,000 people attend the festival. Over 30 volunteers, bakers, and sponsors, including one mom who lost her son to pediatric cancer, came together to make our bake sale happen. We baked over 1,000 cookies and secured donations of bottled water, coffee, hot chocolate, napkins, sugar, creamer, and cups from a local grocery store and bank. We raised nearly $2,000 in one day—everyone felt the festival was the right location, the perfect audience, and we can't wait to do it again at the 5th Annual Carefree Christmas Festival.

seriously short chocolate chip cookies

yield: depending on scoop size and
whether or not nuts are added,
4 to 12 dozen cookies

We love our cookies short—not in stature, but with just the right blend of fat and sugar to melt in your mouth. The shortening here is key: It gives the perfect balance, with the butter adding depth of flavor. This recipe makes a big batch of dough that can be scooped up in any size you want. Just keep an eye on them and adjust the baking time.

2 sticks (½ pound) unsalted butter, at room temperature

1 cup butter-flavored shortening

1¼ cups light brown sugar

1 cup granulated sugar

3 large eggs, at room temperature

1 tablespoon vanilla extract

4 cups all-purpose flour

1½ teaspoons baking soda

2 teaspoons salt

6 cups (2¼ pounds) semi-sweet chocolate chips

3 cups chopped nuts (optional)

- Preheat the oven to 350°F. Line 2 cookie sheets with parchment paper.

- Place the butter, shortening, and sugars in a large mixer bowl and beat until smooth and creamy, about 3 minutes. Add the eggs one at a time, beating after each addition, and the vanilla.

- Place the flour, baking soda, and salt in a separate bowl; mix well and add to the butter mixture. Beat until everything is well incorporated. Scrape down the sides of the bowl, add the chocolate chips, and mix again. Add nuts, if using, and mix again.

- Using a cookie scoop, drop the dough about 2 inches apart on the prepared cookie sheets.

- Transfer to the oven and bake until the cookies begin to brown at the edges, 10 to 12 minutes, rotating the cookie sheets on the oven racks halfway through the baking time. Cool on the cookie sheets for 3 minutes. Transfer to wire racks to cool completely. Repeat with the remaining dough on cool cookie sheets.

- Store in an airtight container for up to 3 days, or freeze for up to 3 months.

inspire ❋ Using photos highlighting children battling cancer, create your own "Kids Who Inspire Us" banner to put faces and stories with the cause. Helping people understand that local kids benefit when we give to national organizations inspires people to give generously and opens up a meaningful conversation about the importance of the event.

michelle sohn's oatmeal chocolate chips

yield: 5 dozen

Three generations of Michelle's family make these cookies: Michelle, her mom, and her son.

2 sticks (½ pound) unsalted butter, at room temperature

1 cup light brown sugar

1 cup granulated sugar

2 large eggs, at room temperature

1 teaspoon vanilla extract

2½ cups quick-cooking oats

2 cups all-purpose flour

1 teaspoon baking powder

1 teaspoon baking soda

½ teaspoon salt

2 cups (12 ounces) chocolate chips

2 cups chopped walnuts (optional)

- Preheat the oven to 350°F. Line 2 cookie sheets with parchment paper

- Place the butter and sugars in a large mixer bowl and beat until smooth and creamy, about 3 minutes. Add the eggs one at a time, beating after each addition, and the vanilla.

- Place the oats, flour, baking powder, baking soda, and salt in a separate bowl; mix well and add to the butter mixture. Beat until everything is well incorporated. Scrape down the sides of the bowl, add the chocolate chips and nuts, if using, and mix again.

- Using a level medium (1½-tablespoon size) cookie scoop, drop the dough about 2 inches apart on the prepared cookie sheets.

- Transfer to the oven and bake until the cookies begin to brown at the edges, 12 to 15 minutes, rotating the cookie sheets on the oven racks halfway through the baking time. Cool on the cookie sheets for 3 minutes. Transfer to wire racks to cool completely. Repeat with the remaining dough on cool cookie sheets.

- Store in an airtight container for up to 3 days, or freeze for up to 3 months.

sally sampson's kitchen sink cookies

yield: 5 dozen cookies

Loaded with yum, these cookies are the creation of Sally Sampson, the genius behind the recipes in the first *Cookies for Kids' Cancer Best Bake Sale Cookbook.* You can put anything in them except the proverbial sink. Nut allergies? Swap them out for extra dried fruit.

2 sticks (½ pound) unsalted butter, at room temperature

½ cup granulated sugar

½ cup light brown sugar

2 large eggs, at room temperature

2 teaspoons vanilla extract

1 cup quick cooking oats

2 cups all-purpose flour

1 teaspoon baking powder

1 teaspoon baking soda

1 teaspoon kosher salt

2 cups (12 ounces) semisweet chocolate chips or butterscotch chips

1 cup dark raisins or dried cranberries

1 cup chopped dried apricots

1 cup lightly toasted walnuts, coarsely chopped

½ cup sweetened flaked coconut

½ cup lightly toasted pumpkin seeds

½ cup lightly toasted sunflower seeds

- Place the butter and sugars in a large mixer bowl and beat until smooth and creamy, about 3 minutes. Add the eggs one at a time, beating after each addition, and the vanilla. Scrape down the sides of the bowl; add the oats, flour, baking powder, baking soda, and salt and mix until everything is well incorporated. Scrape down the sides of the bowl; add the chocolate chips, raisins, apricots, walnuts, coconut, and pumpkin and sunflower seeds. Mix again.

- Cover and refrigerate for at least 1 hour and up to 3 days.

- Preheat the oven to 325°F. Line 2 cookie sheets with parchment paper.

- Using a level medium (1½-tablespoon size) cookie scoop, drop the dough about 2 inches apart on the prepared cookie sheets.

- Transfer the cookie sheets to the oven and bake until the cookies begin to brown at the edges and are still soft in the middle, about 12 minutes, rotating the cookie sheets on the oven racks halfway through the baking time. Cool on the cookie sheets for 3 minutes. Transfer to wire racks to cool completely. Repeat with the remaining dough on cool cookie sheets.

- Store in an airtight container for up to 3 days, or freeze for up to 3 months.

be a considerate good cookie ❀ When offering gluten-free or other allergen-free baked goods: Print recipe cards to attach to each bag of goodies. Moms who are concerned with allergies are more likely to buy something when they can be confident of its ingredients!

cornflake cookies

yield: about 3 dozen cookies

In the United States, we have a long-standing tradition of making cookies with breakfast cereal. They're crunchy, yummy, and fun, and everyone loves them. They're not a breakfast replacement, but they are a fine cookie.

3 cups cornflakes, crushed

1 cup all-purpose flour

1 cup granulated sugar

¾ cup sweetened flaked coconut

½ teaspoon salt

1¼ sticks (5 ounces) unsalted butter, at room temperature

2 tablespoons light corn syrup

1 teaspoon baking soda

1 teaspoon vanilla extract

1 large egg, at room temperature, beaten

- Preheat the oven to 350°F. Line 2 cookie sheets with parchment paper.
- Place the cornflakes, flour, sugar, coconut, and salt in a large bowl and stir to combine.
- Place the butter in a small saucepan and melt over medium heat. Add the corn syrup and cook, stirring, until mixture comes to a boil. Add the baking soda and stir rapidly to blend. When the foam settles, remove from the heat and add the vanilla, stirring to combine.
- Pour the butter mixture over the cornflake mixture and mix thoroughly. Add the egg and stir to combine.
- Press the dough into measured tablespoon mounds against the sides of mixer bowl and place on the prepared cookie sheets, about 2 inches apart.
- Transfer to the oven and bake until the cookies begin to brown at the edges, 7 to 9 minutes, rotating the cookie sheets on the oven racks halfway through the baking time. Cool on the cookie sheets for 3 minutes. Transfer to wire racks and cool completely. Repeat with the remaining dough on cool cookie sheets.
- Store in an airtight container for up to 3 days, or freeze for up to 3 months.

lemon perfection squares

yield: 4 dozen squares

Given a choice between lemon and chocolate, Fraya goes for lemon every time. So it's no wonder these are one of her favorite cookies on the planet. The combo of juice and freshly grated zest in the filling is the key to their sweet-tart citrus punch.

for the crust

2 sticks (½ pound) unsalted butter, at room temperature

2 cups all-purpose flour

½ cup confectioners' sugar

Pinch salt

for the filling

4 large eggs, at room temperature

1¾ cups granulated sugar

¼ cup all-purpose flour

¾ teaspoon baking powder

⅓ cup fresh lemon juice

2 teaspoons freshly grated lemon zest

Confectioners' sugar

- Preheat the oven to 350°F. Line a 9 x 13-inch baking pan with foil.
- **To make the crust.** Place the butter in a mixer bowl and beat until creamy. Add the flour, confectioners' sugar, and salt and beat to combine. Press the dough into the bottom of the prepared pan. Transfer to the oven and bake until set and golden, 20 to 25 minutes.
- **To make the filling:** In a medium bowl, whisk together the eggs, sugar, flour, baking powder, lemon juice, and zest. Pour over the baked crust and return to the oven. Bake until set, 20 to 25 minutes. Cool in the pan on a wire rack. When cool, remove from the pan, cut in 48 squares, and dust with confectioners' sugar.
- Store in the refrigerator for up to 3 days, or freeze for up to 3 months.

Scotch Plains, NJ

JENNIFER DIXON/UNION CATHOLIC HIGH SCHOOL
Scotch Plains, NJ

Union Catholic began raising money for Cookies for Kids' Cancer in 2007, before it officially existed! I learned about Liam through my husband, who had mutual friends with Liam's dad Larry. Liam had just been diagnosed and was only a year older than my son. Our hearts broke, knowing the helpless feeling we have when our own children have even minor medical ailments. My husband helped coordinate a roller hockey tournament and with the help of my school, we ran a "Kisses for Liam" fundraiser. Students spent days bagging handfuls of Hershey's Kisses, attaching a picture of Liam, and selling them for $1. I was overwhelmed not only by the profit we made, but by how much ownership the students took for the project and the pride they had.

When Gretchen hosted her first cookie fundraiser during the winter of 2007, I was amazed and humbled by her energy to give back and move forward for ALL children who were affected by cancer. Cookies for Kids' Cancer started when Union Catholic's Student Movement Against Cancer (SMAC) club was also coming together. Under the leadership of several committed teachers, SMAC has grown to be one of our largest and most active clubs, with about 200 student members who raise funds and awareness for several charities all year. The club holds an annual Cookies for Kids' Cancer event. They use their talents and have created videos, photo montages, and posters to advertise the bake sales. Students love baking and selling their treats while educating peers about the cause. SMAC raises nearly $500 at each bake sale. With minimal direction, students learn leadership skills and take responsibility, while we watch their self-esteem blossom.

I have been so inspired by the service leadership experience this has provided our high school students. My 5-year-old son held a bake sale out of his red wagon last spring. He was so proud to bake his cookies and told everyone he was selling "to help the sick kids." How could you turn him down?! He raised over $100!

BERGER TRUE VALUE HARDWARE
Hawthorne, NY

I first read about Cookies for Kids' Cancer on OXO's website. When I read Liam's story, I felt compelled to help. My husband was diagnosed with a rare form of cancer shortly after we were married, so Liam's story really hit home for us. My husband was treated at Memorial Sloan-Kettering Cancer Center and sometimes we would walk on the pediatric floor and think about how much harder it would be to undergo treatment as a child. Those memories came flooding back when I read about Liam.

What I loved about Cookies for Kids' Cancer was that the idea was so simple—just bake some cookies or your favorite treat. I think that people do want to help, but sometimes they just don't know how. We live in a great community, and I knew our staff and customers would want to help.

We planned our event for a Saturday in December, figuring, everyone bakes at Christmastime anyway. The location was the True Value Hardware Store I own with my brother Chris. To let our customers know what we were up to, we placed flyers in our shopping bags leading up to the big day, blasted our email list, and posted signs around the store. We enlisted other local businesses and bakeries to donate tons of baked goods, and a coffee house donated plenty of hot java. The day before the sale was amazing—I was so excited when the first customer came in, handed over 6 dozen cookies, and thanked us for letting her help. Then, the baked goods just kept coming! All day long customers kept coming in to drop off their special goodies. We started an assembly line and placed the cookies in cello bags with Cookies for Kids' Cancer logo stickers.

The day of the sale, we had Santa Claus at the store to talk to kids, and we set up a crafts station for them. While they were entertained, their parents shopped our bake sale. Our customers loved everything, and we even ended up on the local television news and in the newspaper.

hermits

yield: 6 dozen cookies

You'll hear several ideas about why these soft, spicy cookies are called Hermits, but the one we like best is that they can hide out like hermits (in a cookie jar) for several days and still be soft and yummy. That makes them perfect for bake sales: They can be the first batch you bake and package.

1½ cups dark raisins

½ cup hot coffee

2 sticks (½ pound) unsalted butter, at room temperature

1 cup light brown sugar

2 large eggs, at room temperature

1 teaspoon vanilla extract

2 cups all-purpose flour

¾ teaspoon baking soda

1 teaspoon ground cinnamon

½ teaspoon ground nutmeg

¼ teaspoon ground cloves

¾ cup chopped, pitted dates

1 cup chopped pecans (optional)

- Preheat the oven to 350°F. Line 2 cookie sheets with parchment paper.
- Place the raisins and hot coffee in a bowl to plump the raisins, and set aside. Place the butter and sugar in a large mixer bowl and beat until smooth and creamy, about 3 minutes. Add the eggs one at a time, beating after each addition, and the vanilla.
- Place the flour, baking soda, cinnamon, nutmeg, and cloves in a separate bowl; mix well and add to the butter mixture. Beat until everything is well incorporated. Drain the raisins, discarding liquid. Scrape down the sides of the bowl, add the plumped raisins and the dates, and mix again. Add nuts, if using, and mix again.
- Using a heaping small (2-teaspoon size) cookie scoop, drop the dough about 2 inches apart on the prepared cookie sheets.
- Transfer to the oven and bake until the cookies begin to brown at the edges, 10 to 12 minutes, rotating the cookie sheets on the oven racks

halfway through the baking time. Cool on the cookie sheets for 3 minutes. Transfer to wire racks to cool completely. Repeat with the remaining dough on cool cookie sheets.

- Store in an airtight container for up to 3 days, or freeze for up to 3 months.

tips from top hosts
 **CARA PEARSON + MICHELLE RIDDLE, SANTA CRUZ, CA**

Top 10 Keys to Success for Ladies' Night Out Benefiting
Cookies for Kids' Cancer

1. Buzz about the event!—Facebook, Twitter, and local press make all the difference.
2. Fun, fun, fun—make sure attendees know this is their excuse to put on their LBD (little black dress)!
3. Passion for the cause—don't be afraid to talk about WHY this night out is important.
4. Community involvement—get local businesses to sponsor or be a part of the event.
5. Event location—make it accessible and inviting.
6. Something to take home—swag bags, raffle prizes, and silent auctions are great ways to draw a crowd.
7. Décor—design a night ladies will love: something bright and cheerful.
8. Food—it's not all about cookies. Make sure to have sweets and salties.
9. Music—either a DJ or a great dance list will keep the party going and make it a night to remember.
10. Inspiration—share the stories of local kids in battle or share the story of why Cookies for Kids' Cancer matters to you.

amazingly chewy oatmeal cookies

yield: 6 to 8 dozen cookies, depending on size of scoop

Sometimes we have an idea for how a recipe should come out and we make it three or four times to get it right. Sometimes we nail it on the first try. We knew exactly what kind of oatmeal cookie we wanted—chewy, with just a hint of cinnamon—and we got it right away by using just brown sugar. High-fives on this one.

1 stick (¼ pound) unsalted butter, at room temperature

¾ cup light brown sugar

1 large egg, at room temperature

1 teaspoon vanilla extract

¾ cup all-purpose flour

1½ cups quick-cooking oats

½ teaspoon baking soda

½ teaspoon salt

½ teaspoon ground cinnamon

¾ cup dark raisins

¾ cup chopped walnuts (optional)

- Place the butter and sugar in a large mixer bowl and beat until smooth and creamy, about 3 minutes. Add the egg and the vanilla one at a time, beating after each addition.

- Place the flour, oats, baking soda, salt, and cinnamon in a separate bowl; mix well and add to the butter mixture. Beat until everything is well incorporated. Scrape down the sides of the bowl, add the raisins and nuts, if using, and mix again. Place bowl with dough in the refrigerator and chill for 30 to 60 minutes.

- Preheat the oven to 350°F. Line 2 cookie sheets with parchment paper.

- Using a cookie scoop, drop the dough about 2 inches apart on the prepared cookie sheets.

- Transfer to the oven and bake until the cookies begin to brown at the edges, 10 to 12 minutes, rotating the cookie sheets on the oven racks halfway through the baking time. Cool on the cookie sheets for 5 minutes. Transfer to wire racks to cool completely. Repeat with the remaining dough on cool cookie sheets.

- **baker's note** Baking time will depend on the size of cookie scoop and how long the dough is chilled. Cookies will be browned at the edges and will look slightly moist on top when done. The 5 minutes on the cookie sheet after they come out of the oven ensures they are fully baked.

- Store in an airtight container for up to 3 days, or freeze for up to 3 months.

what to offer ❅ Mason jars filled with cookie ingredients are big hits! Not only are they cute, it's easy to take them home, add the wet ingredients, and have freshly baked cookies. They also make perfect gifts. Hot chocolate and tea mixes in jars do well too.

banana-nut bars

yield: 2 dozen bars

Banana bread is always a big seller at bake sales, but we're all about cookies and bars here, so we set out to make a banana bread stand-in. A frosted bar seemed like a good idea to Jackie, so she ran with it. She captured all the familiar flavors in a moist batter that fills a 9 x 13-inch pan perfectly, is easy to cut, and has frosting.

for the bars

1 stick (¼ pound) unsalted butter, at room temperature

1 cup granulated sugar

2 large eggs, at room temperature

4 very ripe bananas, mashed (about 1½ cups)

½ cup buttermilk

1 teaspoon vanilla extract

2 cups all-purpose flour

½ cup quick-cooking oats

1 teaspoon baking soda

½ teaspoon salt

1 cup chopped walnuts

for the frosting

1½ cups confectioners' sugar

3 tablespoons unsalted butter, at room temperature

3 tablespoons milk

½ teaspoon vanilla extract

- Preheat the oven to 350°F. Generously grease a 9 x 13-inch baking pan.

- **To make the bars:** Place the butter and granulated sugar in a large mixer bowl and beat until smooth and creamy. Add the eggs, one at a time, beating after each addition. Add the bananas, buttermilk, and vanilla and beat well. Scrape down the sides of the bowl and beat again. Place the flour, oats, baking soda, and salt in a separate bowl; mix well. Add to the banana mixture and stir until well combined.

- Pour batter into prepared pan. Top with the walnuts. Transfer to the oven and bake until a toothpick inserted in the center comes out clean, about 30 to 35 minutes. Cool completely in the pan on a wire rack.

banana-nut bars (cont.)

- **To make the frosting:** Place the confectioners' sugar and butter in a bowl and beat until blended. Add milk and vanilla and beat until fluffy, about 2 minutes. Spread the frosting on top of the banana bars and cut into 24 bars.

- Store in the refrigerator for up to 3 days, or freeze for up to 3 months.

community involvement ❈ Consider asking other organizations to come out during your event. Ask the local children's hospital to be a part of the fun and share promotional items or hold a blood or bone marrow match drive to make it easy for people to give even more while they are in the giving spirit.

spread the word ❈ Drop off cookies with radio station morning DJs along with details about your event to get them talking.

dr. la quaglia's carrot-almond drops

yield: about 6 dozen cookies

D r. Michael La Quaglia, pediatric cancer surgeon extraordinaire, has been a Cookies for Kids' Cancer supporter from day one. We asked him what his favorite cookie is, and then we invented this one especially for him. It's the perfect blend of cake and cookie, complete with cream cheese frosting.

for the cookies

1½ sticks (6 ounces) unsalted butter, at room temperature

1 cup light brown sugar

2 large eggs, at room temperature

One 4-ounce jar baby food puréed carrots

2 teaspoons vanilla extract

2 cups all-purpose flour

1 teaspoon ground cinnamon

½ teaspoon baking powder

½ teaspoon baking soda

½ teaspoon salt

2 cups quick-cooking oats

1½ cups shredded carrots

½ cup slivered almonds, toasted (see Tip page 32)

for the frosting

1 stick (¼ pound) unsalted butter, at room temperature

4 ounces cream cheese, at room temperature

1¾ cups confectioners' sugar, sifted

2 teaspoons fresh lemon juice

½ teaspoon vanilla extract

- Preheat the oven to 350°F. Line 2 cookie sheets with parchment paper.
- **To make the cookies:** Place the butter and brown sugar in a large mixer bowl and beat until smooth and creamy, about 3 minutes. Add the eggs, carrot purée, and vanilla, one at a time, beating well after each addition. Scrape down the sides of the bowl. Place the flour, cinnamon, baking powder, baking soda, and salt in a separate bowl, mix well, and with the mixer on low, add to the butter mixture. Beat just to combine. Stir in oats, carrots, and almonds and mix to combine.

- Using a level small (2-teaspoon size) cookie scoop, drop the batter about 2 inches apart on the prepared cookie sheets.
- Transfer to the oven and bake until the edges of the cookies are lightly browned, 10 to 12 minutes, rotating the cookie sheets on the oven racks halfway through the baking time. Cool on the cookie sheets for 3 minutes. Transfer to wire racks and cool completely. Repeat with the remaining dough on cool cookie sheets.
- **To make the frosting:** Place the butter and cream cheese in a large mixer bowl and beat until creamy. Add the sugar and beat until light and fluffy. Add the lemon juice and vanilla and mix until thoroughly combined. Top each cookie with a teaspoon of frosting.
- Store in the refrigerator for up to 3 days, or freeze for up to 3 months.

tip ❀ To toast nuts, preheat the oven to 350°F. Spread the nuts in a single layer on an ungreased baking pan or cookie sheet and bake, stirring once or twice, until golden and fragrant, 10 to 15 minutes (depending on the type of nut).

be prepared ❀ Arrive at your venue at least a few hours early. Plan for worst-case scenarios and make sure you are equipped to handle them. Someone will spill, things will get dropped on the ground, and someone will need change. Bring plenty of napkins to hand out with your goodies, cleaning wipes to take care of any sticky messes, ballpoint pens so people can write donation checks, and don't forget to stop by the bank and pick up some change. Some tens, some fives, and plenty of ones should do the trick!

Justin Sohn, Englewood, NJ

JUSTIN SOHN
Englewood, NJ

I learned about Cookies for Kids' Cancer because my mom works with Gretchen and Larry Witt. When OXO started hosting bake sales to raise money to help kids with cancer, I knew I wanted to get involved. I love to bake (and my friends at school tell me I'm pretty good at it), and I realized that I could do what I love and help kids at the same time. My mom and I have baked, packed, and labeled hundreds of cookies for OXO's bake sales. I even got two of my friends to bake for the bake sales too.

My bar mitzvah is coming up and I decided to honor the occasion by running a 5K and asking my family and friends to sponsor me. All of the money I raise will be donated to Cookies for Kids' Cancer. I can't believe how much money everyone pledged. I feel so lucky to have such generous family and friends who realize how important it is to help other people. My mom and Gretchen have been friends for a long time, and I have learned that it is important to have friends who will help you no matter what. I think my family and friends have set a good example and have taught me to be generous and help out whenever I can.

Not only was I able to celebrate my birthday and good health with my friends, but we also raised money for this amazing organization. It was such a fun and inspirational night that I will definitely do it again next year!

SINDI DIPOMAZIO
Chandler, AZ

I hosted our 2nd annual Cookies for Kids' Cancer bake sale at our neighborhood school. Last year, along with our neighborhood, we hosted our first fund-raising bake sale, sending over $600 to Cookies for Kids' Cancer. I knew then I would keep doing this to help others, especially pediatric cancer patients.
Our second bake sale was situated next to an elementary school, which was a great location for people driving by. Plus, the

kids helping out had a bold sign to attract drivers. All of the treats were packaged in cute Valentine's Day boxes or cello bags tied with ribbon. We offered cookies (of course), Sweethearts, candied apples, brownies, dipped marshmallows, cupcakes, handmade jewelry, handmade hair clips, balloons, single long-stemmed roses, and much more! We also had raffle tickets for spa services donated by local spas.

One highlight of the day was the donation from a group of girls in the neighborhood who call themselves "Make a Change 8." The girls, ranging from 4th to 8th grade, work together to support the community through a variety of projects. They stopped by with a donation of over $100. What an inspiring part of a successful day!

LILLIAN LIN SCHLEIN
New York, NY

I was diagnosed with stage 4 cancer when I was three months old. The tumor was in my adrenal gland and had spread to my liver. The doctors told my parents I had a 5% chance of living. That was in 1969. And although I have health issues as a result of the surgery, chemotherapy, and radiation treatments, I am incredibly lucky and have had a very full life.

I met Gretchen a few years ago at one of the volunteer baking events for Cookies for Kids' Cancer in NYC. When my beautiful, healthy son Julian turned three months old, I could not imagine the thought of him being diagnosed with a disease like this and having to go through vicious chemotherapy and radiation treatments. I wanted to do something more than just volunteer at baking events and cookie sales, but I wasn't sure how to go about it. I came up with the idea to celebrate my upcoming birthday with a private spinning class and asked guests to donate to Cookies for Kids' Cancer in lieu of gifts, dinner, or the cost of the ride. Not everyone is into spinning, and breaking a sweat is definitely not most people's idea of a birthday party, but the fact that it was for an amazing cause got people excited, including me! My birthday celebrations usually involve dressing up and having a celebration with friends. For my 43rd birthday, we had 30 people sweating together in a spin class and raised $3,000 for Cookies for Kids' Cancer. Gretchen spoke before the ride about her son Liam and the organization, which was a great motivator.

As a survivor, Cookies for Kids' Cancer has always been a special organization to me, but it is even more so now that I am a parent.

chocolate chip heath crunch strips

yield: about 5 dozen cookies

We know everyone has a favorite chocolate chip cookie recipe. When you want something new, this is a fantastic option: In addition to the unique toffee flavor, their shape makes them a standout.

2 sticks (½ pound) unsalted butter, at room temperature

⅔ cup light brown sugar

½ cup granulated sugar

1 large egg

1 large egg yolk

2 teaspoons vanilla extract

2 cups all-purpose flour

½ teaspoon baking powder

½ teaspoon salt

1⅓ cups (8 ounces) semi-sweet chocolate chips

½ cup Heath toffee bits

- Preheat the oven to 350°F. Line 2 cookie sheets with parchment paper.
- Place the butter and sugars in a large mixer bowl and beat until smooth and creamy, about 3 minutes. Add the egg, egg yolk, and vanilla one at a time, beating after each addition. Scrape down the sides of the bowl. With the mixer on low, add the flour, baking powder, and salt, beat well and scrape again. Stir in the chocolate chips and toffee bits.
- Divide the dough into quarters. Roll each quarter of the dough between 2 floured sheets of waxed paper into an 8-inch square. Transfer 2 cookie squares to each of the prepared cookie sheets. Transfer to the oven and bake until lightly browned, about 15 to 17 minutes.
- While hot, cut each cookie square in half, then cut each half into eight 1-inch slices. Cool slices on the cookie sheets completely.
- Store in an airtight container for up to 3 days, or freeze for up to 3 months.

faux re-os

yield: about 3½ dozen cookies

The packaged variety is known as America's favorite cookie, but once you make your own you might never go back. Consider a cooler filled with cartons of milk and ice to sell alongside these.

for the cookies

1 stick (¼ pound) unsalted butter, at room temperature

1 cup granulated sugar

1 large egg, at room temperature

1 large egg yolk, at room temperature

1 teaspoon vanilla extract

1½ cups all-purpose flour

½ cup Hershey's Special Dark Unsweetened Cocoa Powder

1 teaspoon baking soda

½ teaspoon salt

¼ teaspoon baking powder

for the filling

6 tablespoons (3 ounces) unsalted butter, at room temperature

3 tablespoons vegetable shortening

2 cups confectioners' sugar, sifted

1 tablespoon vanilla extract

- Preheat the oven to 350°F. Line 2 cookie sheets with parchment paper.

- **To make the cookies:** Place the butter and sugar in a large mixer bowl and beat until smooth and creamy, about 3 minutes. Add the egg, egg yolk, and vanilla one at a time, beating after each addition. Scrape down the sides of the bowl and beat again. Place the flour, cocoa, baking soda, salt, and baking powder in a separate bowl and mix well. With the mixer on low, add the flour mixture and beat until well combined. Scrape down the sides of the bowl and beat again.

- Using a level small (2-teaspoon size) cookie scoop, drop the dough about 2 inches apart on the prepared cookie sheets. With moistened hands, slightly flatten the dough. Transfer to the oven and bake until the edges begin to firm up, 9 minutes, rotating the cookie sheets on the oven racks halfway through the baking time. Cool on the cookie sheets for 3 minutes. Transfer to wire racks and cool completely. Repeat with the remaining dough on cool cookie sheets.

- **To make the filling:** Place the butter and shortening in the bowl of a mixer fitted with a whisk and beat until creamy. On low speed, add the confectioners' sugar and vanilla and beat until combined. Increase the speed of the mixer to high and beat until light and fluffy, 2 to 3 minutes.

- Spread a scant teaspoonful of filling onto each bottom of half of the cookies and place upside down on work surface. Top with remaining cookies, bottom side down. Gently squeeze the cookie sandwiches so filling spreads to the edge.

- Store in an airtight container for up to 3 days, or freeze for up to 3 months.

tips for school events ❋ School events are popular, but there are often rules prohibiting homemade treats due to allergies. Don't let this stop your desire to support Cookies for Kids' Cancer. Ask local bakeries, restaurants, and grocery stores to donate baked goods to your sale.

jackie's chocolate cut-out cookies

yield: about 4 dozen 3-inch cookies

Jackie created this chocolate version of Cut-Outs because her daughter Moya wanted to be sure that "everyone gets to have a cookie that's not too sweet." Two types of chocolate give these scrumptious beauties depth of flavor.

for the cookies

3 ounces unsweetened chocolate

2 sticks (½ pound) unsalted butter, at room temperature

1½ cups granulated sugar

2 large eggs, at room temperature

2 teaspoons vanilla extract

1 tablespoon light corn syrup

4 cups all-purpose flour

½ cup Hershey's Special Dark Unsweetened Cocoa Powder

½ teaspoon salt

for the royal icing

4 cups (about 1 pound) confectioners' sugar

3 tablespoons meringue powder (powdered egg whites)

6 to 8 tablespoons warm water

Assorted icing colors

- **To make the cookies:** Place the unsweetened chocolate in a microwave-safe bowl. Cook on high for 60 seconds, stirring once halfway through. Stir until smooth and the chocolate is completely melted. Let cool for 5 minutes.

- Place the butter and sugar in a large mixer bowl and beat until smooth and creamy, about 3 minutes. Add the eggs, vanilla, and corn syrup one at a time, beating after each addition. Scrape down the sides of the bowl. With the mixer on low, add the flour, cocoa, and salt, beating well. Add the melted chocolate; beat well and scrape again. Divide the dough into 3 disks and flatten slightly. Wrap in plastic wrap and refrigerate for at least 1 hour and up to 2 days, or freeze for up to 2 months.

- Preheat the oven to 350°F. Line 2 cookie sheets with parchment paper.

the classic gotta-haves for a bake sale   41

- Roll out the dough between 2 sheets of waxed paper to a scant ¼-inch thickness. Cut out the dough using cookie cutters and place 1 inch apart on the prepared cookie sheets. Transfer to the oven and bake until the cookies are just beginning to brown on the edges, about 8 to 10 minutes, rotating the cookie sheets on the oven racks halfway through the baking time. Cool on the cookie sheets for 3 minutes. Transfer to wire racks and cool completely. Repeat with the remaining dough on cool cookie sheets.

- **To make the icing:** Place the confectioners' sugar and meringue powder in the bowl of a mixer fitted with a whisk and beat on low speed to blend. Add water, 1 tablespoon at a time, until the mixture is spreadable. Increase the speed of the mixer to high and beat until peaks form, about 6 minutes. Divide the icing among resealable containers (this prevents the icing from hardening). Tint each container of icing your desired color using the icing colors. When ready to decorate, dilute the icing using 1 teaspoon of water at a time until the icing is the consistency of heavy cream. Keep the icings covered if not using. Decorate the cookies as desired.

- Store in an airtight container for up to 10 days, or freeze for up to 3 months.

cute counts ❀ Dress the part. Either buy a Cookies for Kids' Cancer apron to wear during your event or just grab any apron and add a large Cookies logo sticker from the bake sale kit. You'll immediately look like a "Good Cookie"!

jackie's vanilla cut-out cookies

yield: about 4 dozen 3-inch cookies

They are the absolute essence of an all-butter sugar cookie, and Jackie has been making this Vanilla Cut-Out for years. She can honestly say that she's baked not hundreds but thousands of various shaped cookies. As for the decorating, she calls it her Zen cookie-decorating mode: She zones out and just gets into the shape and colors of each individual cookie.

for the cookies

2 sticks (½ pound) unsalted butter, at room temperature

1 cup granulated sugar

2 large eggs, at room temperature

2 teaspoons vanilla extract

1 tablespoon light corn syrup

4 cups all-purpose flour

½ teaspoon salt

for the royal icing

4 cups (about 1 pound) confectioners' sugar

3 tablespoons meringue powder (powdered egg whites)

6 to 8 tablespoons warm water

Assorted icing colors

- **To make the cookies:** Place the butter and sugar in a large mixer bowl and beat until smooth and creamy, about 3 minutes. Add the eggs, one at a time, vanilla, and corn syrup, beating after each addition. Scrape down the sides of the bowl. With the mixer on low, add the flour and salt, beat well, and scrape again. Divide the dough into 3 disks and flatten slightly. Wrap in plastic wrap and refrigerate for at least 1 hour and up to 2 days, or freeze for up to 2 months.

- Preheat the oven to 350°F. Line 2 cookie sheets with parchment paper.

- Roll out the dough between 2 sheets of waxed paper to a scant ¼-inch thickness. Cut out dough using cookie cutters and place 1 inch apart on the prepared cookie sheets. Transfer to the oven and bake until the cookies are just beginning to brown on the edges, about 8 to 10 minutes, rotating the cookie sheets on the oven racks halfway through the baking time. Cool on the cookie sheets for 3 minutes. Transfer to wire racks and cool completely. Repeat with the remaining dough on cool cookie sheets.

- **To make the icing:** Place the confectioners' sugar and meringue powder in the bowl of a mixer fitted with a whisk and beat on low speed to blend. Add water, 1 tablespoon at a time, until the mixture is spreadable. Increase the speed of the mixer to high and beat until peaks form, about 6 minutes. Divide the icing among resealable containers (this prevents the icing from hardening). Tint each container of icing your desired color using the icing colors. When ready to decorate, dilute the icing using 1 teaspoon of water at a time until the icing is the consistency of heavy cream. Keep the icings covered if not using. Decorate the cookies as desired.

- Store in an airtight container for up to 10 days, or freeze for up to 3 months.

get organized ✳ Call on a local Girl Scout or Boy Scout troop to volunteer at your event, and they can earn a patch too. Cookies for Kids' Cancer will send every Scout who helps at a bake sale a Scout patch as a thank-you.

maple doodles

yield: about 7 dozen cookies

Move over, snickerdoodles, you've got some competition. Syrup gives our doodles a distinct maple flavor, and using brown sugar on the outside makes them unique.

for the cinnamon sugar

½ cup light brown sugar

1 tablespoon ground cinnamon

for the cookies

½ cup vegetable shortening

4 tablespoons (2 ounces) unsalted butter, at room temperature

1½ cups granulated sugar

2 large eggs, at room temperature

½ cup pancake syrup

2 teaspoons vanilla extract

3 cups all-purpose flour

1 tablespoon baking powder

½ teaspoon salt

- **To make the cinnamon sugar:** Place the brown sugar and cinnamon in a shallow bowl and mix until combined. Set aside.
- Preheat the oven to 350°F. Line 2 cookie sheet with parchment paper.
- **To make the cookies:** Place the shortening, butter, and granulated sugar in a large mixer bowl and beat until smooth and creamy, about 3 minutes. Add the eggs, one at a time, beating after each addition. Scrape down the sides of the bowl. Add the syrup and vanilla and beat to combine. Place the flour, baking powder, and salt in a separate bowl and mix well. Reduce mixer speed to low and add flour mixture to the butter mixture until well combined.
- To form the cookies: using a small (2-teaspoon size) cookie scoop or heaping teaspoon, roll into balls. Roll the balls in the cinnamon sugar and place 2 inches apart on the prepared cookie sheets. Using your hand or the bottom of a water glass, press down until slightly flattened.

- Transfer to the oven and bake until the cookies begin to brown at the edges, 12 to 14 minutes, rotating the cookie sheets on the oven racks halfway through the baking time. Cool on the cookie sheets for 3 minutes. Transfer to wire racks to cool completely. Repeat with the remaining dough on cool cookie sheets.

- Store in an airtight container for up to 3 days, or freeze for up to 3 months.

community involvement ❀ When asking local businesses for donations, go in person or make a personal phone call. Businesses are often generous but very busy and don't have time to respond to emails. Help them to be Good Cookies with a personal touch.

Charlotte, NC

AMY CHRISTENBURY
Charlotte, NC

Our fourth Cookies for Kids' Cancer bake sale was at Blackhawk Hardware in Charlotte, North Carolina in December. Every year my fundraising partner Lesa and I learn something in order to make the next year even better. We asked another cancer mom to hold a bake sale at another location on the same day. Blackhawk will always be the home of the "original" bake sale—they welcome us every year and love the event—but having two locations helped us reach new people. We like to incorporate the whole community: Kids of all ages come to help bake and hold signs and wear cupcake costumes. High school students earn school service hours for helping bake and volunteer, and we also had a Girl Scout troop help the effort by bringing homemade signs and encouraging people to come to the bake sale. We hope to add more locations each year in each part of our city.

This year was also the fourth year my son Grier battled cancer. Planning events and bake sales allows me to focus on HOPE instead of fear—I know the money raised will help all kids fighting cancer and raise awareness for the lack of funding pediatric cancer receives. I love the planning and the sense of community that comes with every event we have done in the last four years. I love that our BIG annual December bake sale has become a tradition for many families. It has become my favorite part of the holiday season as well. The night before the bake sale is like Christmas Eve to me. I look forward to seeing the volunteers, setting up the event, and knowing the hard work makes a difference. As a mother of a child with cancer I have met so many people who have been impacted by the four words no parent should hear: "Your child has cancer." Cookies for Kids' Cancer has been one of the positives of this unimaginable journey. I look forward to many more bake sales and events that will provide the hope we all need.

Jamestown, PA

MARISSA MILLER
Jamestown, PA

Three years ago, when I was a sophomore in high school, my mother read an article to me that she discovered in a magazine about Cookies for Kids' Cancer. The second she read it, I fell completely in love. At only 16, I had inherited an amazing talent from my family—baking. This was my chance to put my baking skills to good work.

My mother and her sisters are well known for the delicious things they can create in the kitchen. Since I was born, it was inevitable that I wasn't only going to be a baker, but I would love baking! I knew this was my opportunity to combine my love for baking and children. I held a small bake sale that year and raised $200.

As seniors in high school, my twin brother Tanner and I decided to support Cookies for Kids' Cancer again. We presold 35 trays of cookies in our community for the Christmas holiday and received donations from local grocery stores and companies to help fund our project. With the help of friends and our parents, we arrived at our high school cafeteria and began baking. We baked for ten hours straight, made over 3,000 cookies and successfully did not burn or drop a single cookie!

We delivered all of our trays the very next day, receiving just as many compliments on the cause as we did the cookies. Through our sales we raised $751.79. We absolutely loved baking for this cause and we loved even more that we were able to spread the word about Cookies for Kids' Cancer.

In return, Cookies has impacted my life even more than I could have asked. As I was looking into what I wanted to study in college, my parents asked me, "If you could do anything at all for the rest of your life, what would it be?" Without hesitation, I replied, "I'd love to promote Cookies for Kids' Cancer." It really is my dream to be able to promote something so incredible, and I hope that I can someday make an even bigger impact or share the love I have for this cause with others.

tips from top hosts
✳ TRISHA SHEPHARD, AUSTIN, TX

Bake Sales Are Bigger in Texas—Tips for Going Big!

- With a dozen locations across Austin, we needed a lot of signs and banners. We enlisted a local children's charitable works organization to paint signs. The kids had a great time, and it was just one more way to raise awareness throughout the community. We enlisted the same group to help us with the packaging of cookies.
- We asked several local shops to offer our cookies in exchange for donations at their checkout counter. This had a great return on effort, with no volunteers or setup required.
- We solicited mommy bloggers and food bloggers, local publications, and radio stations for coverage. We secured blog coverage, radio air time, a radio PSA, a feature in a local magazine, and ads in neighborhood newsletters.
- The biggest hits at our family fun festival were cookie decorating and sand art. Other activities included face painting, bounce houses, hula hoops, slot cars, balloon artists, and performances by children's musicians. Some activities were donated. Those that were not donated in full were sponsored by local businesses. We sold tickets for most activities.
- The Girls' Night Out was held on a Wednesday evening, a less expensive night to hold an event, in order to have the cost of the space, food, and setup donated. We charged $50 for tickets and offered 25 exciting silent auction packages and six raffles.
- The biggest hit of our Girls' Night Out was hiding a valuable gift card in a box of cupcakes at the bake sale table! The ladies went crazy for this, and the boxes sold out within minutes of our announcement. This is a must-do at any event!
- We offered sponsorships that included recognition on our volunteer T-shirts, Girls' Night Out swag bags, and print and radio ads, as well as our blog, FB, and Twitter, in order to bring in cash donations.

seriously chocolate

chocolate towers

yield: 2 dozen cookies

Chocolate? Check. Impressive? Check. Easy? Absolutely. Slice-and-bake cookies make these stacks a make-ahead treat ready for a bake sale or a dinner party. The ganache (French for chocolate filling) adds a creamy intensity to the overall chocolate experience.

for the cookies

1 stick (¼ pound) unsalted butter, at room temperature

½ cup granulated sugar

½ cup light brown sugar

1 large egg, at room temperature

1 tablespoon vanilla extract

1¼ cups all-purpose flour

⅔ cup unsweetened cocoa powder

½ teaspoon baking soda

½ teaspoon salt

½ teaspoon ground cinnamon

for the sour cream ganache

1 cup (6 ounces) semi-sweet chocolate chips

½ cup reduced-fat sour cream, at room temperature

1 teaspoon vanilla extract

¼ cup confectioners' sugar

- **To make the cookies:** Place the butter and sugars in a large mixer bowl and beat until smooth and creamy, about 3 minutes. Add the egg and vanilla. Beat to blend, then scrape down the sides of the bowl and mix again.

- Place the flour, cocoa powder, baking soda, and salt in a bowl; mix well and add to the butter mixture. Beat until everything is well incorporated. Scrape down the sides of the bowl, and mix again.

- Form the dough into two 10-inch logs, wrap in plastic wrap, and refrigerate for at least 3 hours and up to 3 days.

- Preheat the oven to 350°F. Line 2 cookie sheets with parchment paper.

- Slice chilled logs of the dough in ¼-inch thick slices and place 1 inch apart on the prepared cookie sheets.

- Transfer to the oven and bake until the cookies are just firm at the edges, 7 to 9 minutes, rotating the cookie sheets on the oven racks halfway through the baking time. Cool on the cookie sheets for 3 minutes. Transfer to wire racks to cool completely. Repeat with the remaining dough on cool cookie sheets.

- **To make the ganache:** Place the chocolate chips in a medium microwave-safe bowl and place in microwave. Heat, stirring every 30 seconds until melted. Gently stir in sour cream and vanilla until well blended. Stir in the confectioners' sugar. Place in a heavyweight zip-top bag.

- **To assemble the towers:** Snip corner from bag. Pipe dollops of ganache on cooled cookies and stack 3 high. Refrigerate for at least 30 minutes and up to 1 day. Do not freeze.

spread the word ❀ Create a Facebook page or Facebook event to keep people posted on details as you plan. Or if your town has a patch.com site, post on the scrolling events page. Start early, with updated reminders and enticing messages.

chocolate pillows

yield: about 8 dozen cookies

Fraya's grandmother was a baker in a small Illinois town, where she made these cookies. After Fraya searched for decades, she found the recipe in an old cardboard box hidden behind some cookbooks. One bite of this creamy milk chocolate–filled cookie took her back to being 8 years old in a nanosecond. Jackie suggested adding cocoa to the dough as an experiment, and it's just as good as the original.

3 sticks (¾ pound) unsalted butter, at room temperature

1 cup granulated sugar

½ teaspoon salt

2 large eggs, at room temperature

1 tablespoon vanilla extract

3⅓ cups all-purpose flour

2 tablespoons Hershey's Special Dark Unsweetened Cocoa Powder (optional)

5 Hershey's chocolate bars (1.7 ounces each)

Sprinkles

- Preheat the oven to 375°F. Line 2 cookie sheets with parchment paper.
- Place the butter, sugar, and salt in a large mixer bowl. Beat until smooth and creamy, about 3 minutes. Add the eggs one at a time, beating after each addition, and the vanilla.
- Slowly add the flour and cocoa powder (if using), beating until well incorporated. Scrape down the sides of the bowl and mix again. Divide the dough in half.
- Place dough in a cookie press fitted with zig-zag strip template. Squeeze dough onto prepared cookie sheets in a strip the length of the cookie sheet. Continue piping until the first half of the dough is used.
- Separate each chocolate bar into 3 strips lengthwise. Place the chocolate on the dough. Pipe remaining half of the dough over the chocolate. Top with sprinkles.

chocolate pillows (cont.)

- Transfer to the oven and bake until the cookies begin to brown slightly at the edges, 12 to 15 minutes, rotating the cookie sheets on the oven racks halfway through the baking time. Cut strips in 1½-inch pieces on the cookie sheets while still warm. Cool on the cookie sheets.

- Store in an airtight container for up to 3 days, or freeze for up to 3 months.

be prepared ❀ Have a "leftovers" plan. No one wants leftovers, but it's smart to plan ahead. There are several approaches. One way to keep raising funds is to have local offices bid for the leftovers—the highest bidder gets everything that's left over. Another option is to think of community service options in your area: local fire departments, police precincts, soup kitchens, or churches would all appreciate the generosity. Always include a flyer about Cookies for Kids' Cancer to keep spreading the word.

Olney, MD

HANNAH SAN SEBASTIAN
Olney, MD

My name is Hannah San Sebastian, and I'm 12 years old. For my bat-mitzvah project, I raised money for Cookies for Kids' Cancer. I heard about this cause when my mother's friend held some bake sales for Cookies for Kids' Cancer. I did a little research and found this cause "irresistible"! I made it my goal to hold 6 bake sales. I have already held 3 and will hold 3 more in the next three months! I am extremely proud to say that I've raised $1,000 so far!

I have learned so much with this cause. I have learned that it's important to get things—like baking cookies—done in advance and to manage my time well. I've learned that it's important to have relationships with businesses. I have learned how to contact people and businesses to get what I need. I have learned that I'm a very good saleswoman and am able to convince people to give more than they normally would by letting them know that the children are grateful for any donation. I have learned the importance of thanking people and being enthusiastic about what they contribute. But most importantly, I have learned what a giving, kind, amazing community I live in with people making such generous donations and helping out any way they can, which I realize is such an extraordinary thing to know.

New York, NY

MARY CANNON
New York, NY

Liam Witt and my daughter were best friends, inseparable since they were three. When he lost his battle, we were devastated. As the date that would have been his 7th birthday approached, we needed to commemorate the bright, funny boy who asked endless questions and gave countless hugs.

The plan: a Cookies for Kids' Cancer bake sale. Our preschool, Chelsea Day School, partnered with Apple Seeds, an indoor play space that was one of Liam's favorite hangouts, to hold a one-day, three-location bake sale.

After selling all morning at school, we moved to a big tent by the famous Flatiron Building in New York City. (Meanwhile, Apple Seeds continued their all-day bake sale.) To appeal to Manhattan pedestrians, we spent weeks before the sale asking neighborhood bakeries and restaurants to donate sweets. Having this "professional" inventory provided the substantial quantities we needed and plenty of irresistible options.

While our three-location bake sale generated more cash than we expected, the bulk of the money we raised actually didn't require flour or sugar. We garnered thousands of dollars by emailing relatives and friends, explaining what we were doing and why, and directing them to our giving page on the Cookies website.

After years of feeling helpless while Liam suffered, it was empowering to simply "do," our children included. Initially a bit timid, they quickly got the hang of explaining we were raising money to cure pediatric cancer. Boy, can a cute six-year-old bring in the bucks! There were smiles all around. In addition to a crash course in math (nothing beats having to make change), our kids internalized a critical lesson: Each one of us can—and should—make a difference.

Early on, we decorated our tent with orange balloons because that was Liam's favorite color. As we finished cleaning up, somehow a bunch worked themselves free and started soaring up to the heavens, to Liam. My dear friend Gretchen, Liam's mom and the Cookies founder, stood still and watched, as did the rest of us. As the balloons floated higher, our tears fell. In the midst of the busy evening commute, it seemed completely quiet. The orange balloons got smaller against the blue May sky. We were filled with sadness. . . and hope.

perfect chocolate crinkles

yield: 5 dozen cookies

A family favorite for years, crinkles are always in demand at Jackie's, especially by her husband. When they're warm, these taste just like the best cup of hot chocolate you've ever had.

1 stick (¼ pound) unsalted butter, at room temperature

2 cups granulated sugar

4 ounces unsweetened baking chocolate, melted and cooled slightly

4 large eggs, at room temperature

2 teaspoons vanilla extract

2½ cups all-purpose flour

2 teaspoons baking powder

½ teaspoon salt

Confectioners' sugar

- Place the butter and sugar in a large mixer bowl and beat until smooth and creamy, about 3 minutes. Add the melted chocolate and beat to blend completely. Add the eggs one at a time, beating after each addition, and the vanilla.

- Place the flour, baking powder, and salt in a separate bowl; mix well and add to the butter mixture. Beat until everything is well incorporated. Scrape down the sides of the bowl and mix again. Refrigerate for 4 hours and up to 3 days.

- Preheat the oven to 350°F. Line 2 cookie sheets with parchment paper.

- Using a level small (2-teaspoon size) cookie scoop, scoop the dough into the confectioners' sugar and roll to coat heavily. Place 2 inches apart on the prepared cookie sheets. Transfer to the oven and bake 10 to 12 minutes, until just set, rotating the cookie sheets on the oven racks halfway through the baking time.

- Cool on the cookie sheets for 3 minutes. Transfer to wire racks to cool completely. Repeat with the remaining dough on cool cookie sheets.

- Store in an airtight container for 1 day, or freeze for up to 3 months.

scoops of rocky road

yield: 4 dozen cookies

We love taking easily recognizable dishes and turning them into something else with the same flavors—hence a cookie that tastes like a scoop of ice cream. You need to plan ahead to make these, because the dough chills for at least 8 hours.

1¾ cups all-purpose flour

1½ teaspoons baking powder

¼ teaspoon salt

4 ounces unsweetened chocolate, coarsely chopped

⅓ cup vegetable oil

1¾ cups granulated sugar

4 large eggs, at room temperature

2 teaspoons vanilla extract

¾ cup semi-sweet chocolate chips

½ cup chopped almonds, toasted (see Tip page 32)

1¼ cups mini marshmallows

- Place the flour, baking powder, and salt in a large mixer bowl; mix well.
- Place chopped chocolate and oil in a heavy saucepan over low heat. Heat, stirring occasionally, until the chocolate is melted. Remove from the heat and stir in the sugar. Add the eggs, one at a time, stirring after each addition. Stir in the vanilla.
- Add the chocolate mixture to the flour mixture in the large bowl. Beat until everything is well incorporated. Scrape down the sides of the bowl, add the chocolate chips and nuts and mix again. Refrigerate for at least 8 hours and up to 3 days.
- Preheat the oven to 350°F. Line 2 cookie sheets with parchment paper.
- Using a medium (1½-tablespoon size) cookie scoop, drop the dough about 2 inches apart on the prepared cookie sheets. Transfer to the oven and bake 8 minutes. Remove from the oven, place 3 mini marshmallows on each cookie, and return to the oven. Bake for 3 minutes longer,

until just firm in center and marshmallows are just melting. Cool on the cookie sheets for 1 minute. Transfer to wire racks to cool completely. Repeat with the remaining dough on cool cookie sheets.

- Store in an airtight container for up to 3 days, or freeze for up to 3 months.

what to offer ✻ Set up a festive table decorated with balloons that display Cookies for Kids' Cancer "goodies." Include cookbooks, bracelets, aprons, and T-shirts. Create curb appeal and offer a "door prize" for one lucky winner.

be prepared ✻ Offer something to drink: lemonade when it's hot, cider or hot chocolate when it's cold . . . This is a quick way to draw people to your table!

everyday skinny mints

yield: about 8 dozen cookies

Why everyday? Because the other ones are only available once a year.

for cookies

2 sticks (½ pound) unsalted butter, at room temperature

¾ cup granulated sugar

2½ cups all-purpose flour

½ cup confectioners' sugar

⅓ cup unsweetened cocoa powder

¼ teaspoon salt

1 teaspoon peppermint extract

½ teaspoon vanilla extract

for coating

2 cups (12 ounces) semi-sweet chocolate chips

½ cup vegetable shortening

- **To make the cookies:** Place the butter and granulated sugar in a mixer bowl and beat until smooth and creamy, about 3 minutes.
- Place the flour, confectioners' sugar, cocoa powder, and salt in a bowl; mix well and add to the butter mixture. Beat until everything is well incorporated. Add the peppermint and vanilla extracts, scrape down the sides of the bowl, and mix again.
- Form the dough into two 12-inch logs, wrap in plastic wrap, and refrigerate for at least 1 hour and up to 3 days.
- Preheat the oven to 350°F. Line 2 cookie sheets with parchment paper.
- Cut chilled logs of the dough in ¼-inch thick slices and place 1 inch apart on the prepared cookie sheets.
- Transfer to the oven and bake until the cookies are just firm at the edges, 12 to 14 minutes, rotating the cookie sheets on the oven racks halfway through the baking time. Cool on the cookie sheets for 3 minutes. Transfer to wire racks to cool completely. Repeat with the remaining dough on cool cookie sheets.

- **To make the coating**: Line cold cookie sheets with waxed paper. Combine the chocolate and shortening in microwave-safe bowl. Microwave on high, stirring every 45 to 60 seconds, until the chocolate is melted and mixture has the consistency of thick heavy cream.

- Using a fork, dip the cooled cookies, one at a time, in the melted chocolate. Drain well and transfer to waxed paper. Refrigerate for 15 to 20 minutes to set the chocolate. Repeat with the remaining cookies, reheating chocolate as necessary to keep it at the right consistency.

- Store in the refrigerator for up to 3 days, or freeze for up to 3 months.

be prepared ❈ Label baskets with the type of baked goods inside—people like to know what they're buying, and it saves you from answering the same questions over and over. Place card holders are an adorable way to display labels and tags on the baskets.

chocolate brownie drops

yield: 5 dozen cookies

Perfect for when you just can't decide whether you want a cookie or a brownie—now you can have both in one bite! Melting the butter gives them their glossy sheen.

1½ sticks (6 ounces) unsalted butter, at room temperature

1½ cups granulated sugar

½ cup light brown sugar

4 large eggs, at room temperature

1 tablespoon vanilla extract

1¾ cups all-purpose flour

1 cup Dutch process cocoa powder

1 teaspoon salt

½ teaspoon baking powder

1 cup (6 ounces) bittersweet chocolate chips

- Place the butter and sugars in a microwave-safe bowl. Cook on high for 60 seconds, stirring once halfway through. Stir until smooth and the butter is completely melted. Cook the butter-sugar mixture for 20 seconds more, just until hot (110°F to 120°F). Stir the mixture until slightly shiny looking. (This heating dissolves more of the sugar, which yields a shiny top crust on your cookies.) Cool for 5 minutes.

- Place the eggs in a large mixer bowl and beat until light yellow and creamy, about 3 minutes. Add the butter-sugar mixture and vanilla, beating well to combine. Place the flour, cocoa, salt, and baking powder in a separate bowl. With the mixer on low, add to butter mixture. Beat until everything is well combined. Scrape down the sides of the bowl, add the chocolate chips, and stir to combine. Cover and chill dough for 1 hour or up to 2 days.

- Preheat the oven to 350°F. Line 2 cookie sheets with parchment paper.

- Using a level small (2-teaspoon size) cookie scoop, drop the dough about 2 inches apart on the prepared cookie sheets.

- Transfer to the oven and bake until the cookies begin to firm around the edges, 11 to 13 minutes, rotating the cookie sheets on the oven racks halfway through the baking time. Cool on the cookie sheets for 3 minutes. Transfer to wire racks and cool completely. Repeat with the remaining dough on cool cookie sheets.

- Store in an airtight container for up to 3 days, or freeze for up to 3 months.

pricing—our philosophy: ❀ Don't put a price on your baked goods. Instead, encourage your customers with the motto: "Give what you can, take what you want." Make sure every volunteer is ready to say those eight simple words and then explain how every dollar makes a difference in the world of pediatric cancer because Cookies for Kids' Cancer uses the money to fund research for new treatments for kids fighting cancer. Every dollar counts.

chocolate meringues

yield: about 4 dozen cookies

Crispy on the outside with a center that's a chewy, chocolaty treat. It's easy to pipe lots and lots of any fanciful shape with a large pastry or plastic bag and a star tip. Or simply drop batter using a small cookie scoop.

3 ounces bittersweet chocolate, cut into chunks	3 large egg whites, at room temperature
⅔ cup confectioners' sugar	½ teaspoon fresh lemon juice
3 tablespoons unsweetened cocoa powder	¼ teaspoon salt
	½ cup granulated sugar

- Preheat the oven to 200°F. Line 2 cookie sheets with parchment paper.
- Place the chocolate in a small food processor and pulse until finely ground.
- Sift together the confectioners' sugar and cocoa in a medium bowl.
- Place the egg whites, lemon juice, and salt in the bowl of a mixer fitted with a whisk and beat until foamy. With the mixer running, add the granulated sugar, 1 tablespoon at a time. Increase the speed to high and beat until stiff peaks form. Fold the confectioners' sugar mixture and the chocolate into the egg whites until well combined.
- Spoon the batter into a disposable pastry bag fitted with a large star tip and pipe about 1 tablespoon of the batter 1 inch apart, on the prepared cookie sheets.
- Transfer to the oven and bake for 1 hour. Turn the oven off and leave the meringues in the oven for at least an additional hour.
- Store in an airtight container for up to 3 days, or freeze for up to 3 months.

Austin, TX

TRISHA SHEPARD
Austin, TX

I became familiar with Cookies for Kids' Cancer through my sister-in-law, who helped orchestrate an amazingly successful bake sale in Richmond, Virginia. As I began to follow the Witts' story, Liam found a very special place in my heart. I have two young boys of my own, and my heart ached with thoughts of the grief that Gretchen was experiencing, a grief no mother should endure, and the battle that Liam was fighting, a battle no toddler should even be familiar with.

I felt helpless sitting around full of heartache for the families experiencing childhood cancer, and feeling so incredibly blessed to have my own boys. The "busy" in my life came to a halt when I asked myself what it would mean to me, if I were in Gretchen's shoes, to have someone give up a small piece of their life, a slice of their own time, to hold a fundraiser.

I told everyone I knew about Cookies for Kids' Cancer and asked them how they could help me pull off a fundraiser with a goal of $25,000. With a committee of five other moms, and the support of the businesses and families in our community, we planned a fundraiser to reach a wide demographic. Our fundraiser had three components: a city-wide bake sale with a dozen locations throughout Austin, a family fun festival held at a local outdoor shopping mall, and a Girls' Night Out and Silent Auction. Even as wildfires ripped through our area and fundraisers popped up on every corner to help those victims, people were still willing to give to our cause as well. Our events raised $30,000 and awareness for Cookies for Kids' Cancer. My favorite moment of the entire event was meeting one of our volunteers whose son had been recently diagnosed with cancer. He expressed how much our efforts meant to him, and that was all I needed to hear to know that we'd do it again next year!

Granger, IN

HALEY MEEKHOF
Granger, IN

I love this organization and the fun way that it raises money for such an important cause. I hosted a bake sale through my school's Student Council and National Honor Society.

We baked for 2 days to prepare for the sale. Thursday went fabulously, and we made seven different recipes, all double batches. Friday was a different story. In a matter of hours, the group of well-intended boys ruined a double batch of white chocolate macadamia nut cookies, a double batch of brownies, and left a batch of Rice Krispies treats to freeze.

Despite baking setbacks, the bake sale went perfectly. We sold at one of the busiest sections of our mall on a Saturday and Sunday from 12 to 4. Saturday as we were setting up, we already had a crowd eager to buy our cookies. We made 12 different recipes. Our best sellers were our Peanut Butter Blossom Cookies and the Fluffernutter Blondie Bars, though the kids loved the Rice Krispies Treats and parents getting cookies for their kids loved the Fun Face Cookies. Saturday was such a rush—we sold three-fourths of everything we had made. We had a lot of fun and made many more things to sell! Businesses were very generous and eager to help and we got ingredients donated, T-shirts, stickers with the logos on them, a banner, and 600 bags to package. It all went very smoothly!

Next year I will be a senior and am going to organize another fundraiser for Cookies for Kids' Cancer. Then I'll pass it on to an upcoming junior. I plan on the organizations holding a bake sale for Cookies for Kids' Cancer every year. Now that I have done it once, I know next year will be ten times better and we will raise so much more. We met our goal of $1,000, which made me so happy! Thank you for creating this organization because I know so many people whose lives are affected because of cancer and I know how important it is to have new treatments.

deep chocolate cherry cashew cookies

yield: about 4 dozen cookies

A longtime supporter, Jennifer Perillo dedicated these scrumptious bites to Cookies for Kids' Cancer, on her blog *In Jennie's Kitchen*. The deep chocolate flavor in these chewy cookies comes from bittersweet chips and cocoa powder, intensified by instant espresso (a trick professional bakers use). Cherries and cashews make them utterly and sublimely unique.

1½ cups (9 ounces) bittersweet chocolate chips divided	¾ cup all-purpose flour
	½ cup unsweetened cocoa powder
1 stick (¼ pound) unsalted butter, at room temperature	1 teaspoon instant espresso granules
2 large eggs, at room temperature	½ teaspoon salt
1 cup granulated sugar	1 cup chopped cashews, toasted (see Tip page 32)
1 teaspoon vanilla extract	1 cup dried sour cherries

- Preheat the oven to 350°F. Line 2 cookie sheets with parchment paper.

- Place 1 cup of chocolate chips and butter in a microwave-safe bowl. Cook on high for 60 seconds, stirring once halfway through. Stir until smooth and chocolate is completely melted. Let cool for 5 minutes.

- Place the eggs and sugar in a large mixer bowl and beat until thick and pale yellow. Add the vanilla and cooled chocolate mixture and beat to combine.

- Place the flour, cocoa, espresso, and salt in a separate bowl and mix well. Using a wooden spoon, fold the flour mixture into the chocolate mixture until just combined, being careful to not overmix. Stir in the remaining ½ cup chocolate chips, the cashews, and the cherries.

- Using a heaping small (2-teaspoon size) cookie scoop, drop the dough about 2 inches apart on the prepared cookie sheets.

- Transfer to the oven and bake until the cookies begin to brown at the edges, 12 to 14 minutes, rotating the cookie sheets on the oven racks halfway through the baking time. Cool on the cookie sheets for 3 minutes. Transfer to wire racks and cool completely. Repeat with the remaining dough on cool cookie sheets.

- Store in an airtight container for up to 3 days, or freeze for up to 3 months.

what to offer ❋ Stick it on a stick: It's quite the trend when it comes to baking cookies, cupcakes, brownies, and more. Kids most especially love cake pops, and moms love how perfectly portable they are. Baked goods on a stick are both adorable and practical. Whether it's a cookie, a brownie, or a mini cupcake, putting it on a stick makes it perfectly positioned to eat on the go.

cute counts ❋ Create signs that read "Kids Helping Kids" to drive home the mission of the event, then have kids, tweens, and teens from your volunteers' families holding the signs to attract a crowd to your event.

everyone can have a cookie

(allergy-specific cookies)

flourless peanut butter cookies

gluten-free

yield: about 4 dozen cookies

Peanuts and peanut butter pack extra peanutiness into these flour-less cookies, and their saltiness is the perfect balance to the brown sugar. For a sure bake sale sellout, take them to the next level by dunking half of each cookie into melted chocolate.

1¾ cups natural-style creamy peanut butter, at room temperature

1½ cups light brown sugar

2 large eggs, at room temperature

2 teaspoons baking soda

¾ cup coarsely chopped cocktail peanuts

Chocolate sprinkles (optional)

- Preheat the oven to 350°F. Line 2 cookie sheets with parchment paper.

- Place the peanut butter, sugar, eggs, and baking soda in a large mixer bowl and beat until smooth and creamy, about 3 minutes. Stir in the chopped peanuts.

- Using a heaping small (2-teaspoon size) cookie scoop, drop the dough about 1⅓ inches apart on the prepared cookie sheets. Top cookies with chocolate sprinkles, if using.

- Transfer to the oven and bake until the edges of the cookies are lightly browned, 10 to 12 minutes, rotating the cookie sheets on the oven racks halfway through the baking time. Cool on the cookie sheets for 5 minutes. Transfer to wire racks and cool completely. Repeat with the remaining dough on cool cookie sheets.

- Store in an airtight container for up to 3 days, or freeze for up to 3 months.

booster balls

nut-free

yield: about 4 dozen cookies

Wheat germ takes the place of nuts in these meltingly delicious faux Mexican wedding cookies. We call them Booster Balls for the energy boost you get from the wheat germ.

2 sticks (½ pound) unsalted butter, at room temperature

½ cup granulated sugar

1½ teaspoons vanilla extract

1¾ cups all-purpose flour

1 cup wheat germ

1 cup confectioners' sugar

1 teaspoon ground cinnamon

- Preheat the oven to 400°F. Line 2 cookie sheets with parchment paper.
- Place the butter and granulated sugar in a mixer bowl and beat until smooth and creamy, about 3 minutes. Add the vanilla and beat well to combine.
- Place the flour and wheat germ in a separate bowl; mix well and add to the butter mixture gradually. Beat until everything is well incorporated and dough is smooth. Scrape down the sides of the bowl and mix again.
- Using a heaping small (2-teaspoon size) cookie scoop, drop the dough about 2 inches apart on the prepared cookie sheets. Transfer to the oven and bake until the cookies begin to brown at the edges, 12 to 14 minutes, rotating the cookie sheets on the oven racks halfway through the baking time. Cool on the cookie sheets for 3 minutes. Transfer to wire racks to cool completely. Repeat with the remaining dough on cool cookie sheets.
- Whisk the confectioners' sugar and cinnamon together in a medium-sized bowl. Roll cooled cookies in cinnamon-sugar mix.
- Store in an airtight container for up to 3 days, or freeze for up to 3 months.

Charlotte, NC, 5K Race

ABBEY ROGERS
Charlotte, NC

As a sophomore in the International Baccalaureate program at Myers Park High School, I was asked to complete a personal project that gave me the opportunity to research and create a product of the topic of my choice. For my project, I wanted to do something that would make a difference, so I chose to start a Cookies for Kids' Cancer 5K Race and Bake Sale in Charlotte, North Carolina.

I was inspired by a family friend, Grier Christenbury, who was diagnosed at age 2½ with stage 4 cancer. Since his diagnosis, Grier and his family fight hard every day to battle this terrible cancer. Grier is an amazing little boy, enduring endless rounds of chemo, needles, medicines—and keeps on fighting each day. His determination and spirit inspired me to do what I can to help raise awareness and find a cure for pediatric cancer so other families do not have to endure this difficult circumstance.

The first annual Cookies for Kid's Cancer 5K Race and Bake Sale took place on St. Patrick's Day. On this glorious spring day, we had over 350 runners and raised over $14,000. Young and old came out to support the cause by opening up their hearts and their wallets. I continue to be overwhelmed by the generosity and commitment of local businesses, volunteers, friends, and family—this event was a success because of their concern and support for children like Grier. The event required countless hours of planning, follow-up, and organization for 6 months, but I can say that the life lessons I take with me from this experience are invaluable. I look forward to next year's event being bigger and better than this year!

Richmond, VA

WENDY MARTIN AND TEAM
Richmond, VA

Go big. That's my advice for anyone considering a Cookies for Kids' Cancer bake sale.

Why? Because it's surprisingly easy to do.

Richmond, Virginia, is now gearing up for its third annual city-wide bake sale. The first went from "idea" to "event" in 20 days and was Cookies for Kids' Cancer's highest-grossing sale. Both of our first sales exceeded $30,000.

In our second year, our small team modified our bake sale model. The first year we secured all bake sale sites; provided each with hundreds of cookies, hand-painted table banners, and volunteers; and then collected and counted all the money.

By the second year, we realized all that effort simply wasn't necessary. In every community there are tons of people who hate pediatric cancer and are just waiting for a simple chance to strike back. For our first sale, we went out and found some of those people. By our second sale, even more found *us*.

For year two, we again solicited a donation from Jacqueline's Gourmet Cookies of dough for thousands of cookies. Our first sale taught us that we needed an *industrial* bakery to bake and package that many cookies. Via email, I connected with John Fernandez, owner of local Daystar Desserts.

Tears welled in my eyes when this complete stranger and father of two enthusiastically called me to say that, for him, baking and packaging 16,000 cookies was "not a big sacrifice."

This is "the "yin-yang" of pediatric cancer. For every family randomly stricken by cancer's powerful blows, there are random strangers eager to volunteer to donate their powerful talents in direct opposition. For a while I called that "a miracle." Now I just call it "a fact." I suppose it's a *miraculous* fact.

From there it was easy: We used social media to tell our community, "We're having a city-wide Cookies for Kids' Cancer bake sale. Notify us of your bake sale location no later than one month in advance and you'll get at least 500 cookies (in packs of three), be included in our publicity blitz, and the photo of any child who inspired your sale will be included in the event poster provided to all sites."

Groups of families, Scout troops, and service organizations soon gobbled up our entire cookie donation. Just one month later, a flurry of thirty checks from all over metropolitan Richmond were in the mail to Cookies for Kids' Cancer.

mandel bread

dairy-free

yield: 7 dozen cookies

M andel bread is biscotti's Eastern European cousin. Typical of Jewish desserts served after meat meals, this recipe has no milk products in it, so anyone who's lactose-intolerant can enjoy it too.

½ cup vegetable oil

3 large eggs, at room temperature

¾ cup granulated sugar

½ teaspoon vanilla extract

1 tablespoon fresh lemon juice

3 cups all-purpose flour

1½ teaspoons baking powder

¼ teaspoon baking soda

¼ teaspoon salt

2 cups coarsely chopped walnuts

Chocolate chips (optional)

- Preheat the oven to 350°F. Line a cookie sheet with parchment paper.
- Place the oil, eggs, sugar, vanilla, and lemon juice in a mixer bowl and beat until smooth.
- Place the flour, baking powder, baking soda, and salt in a separate bowl; mix well and add to the egg mixture. Beat until everything is well incorporated. Scrape down the sides of the bowl, add the nuts, and mix again.
- Using cold, wet hands, form the dough into 3 balls and then shape each ball into a 12-inch log. Place the logs about 3 inches apart on the prepared cookie sheet. Transfer to the oven and bake until the tops begin to crack, 20 to 25 minutes. Set aside to cool for 10 minutes.
- Reduce the oven temperature to 325°F. Transfer the baked logs to a cutting board and using a very sharp straight-edged knife, slice the logs on a slight diagonal, about ⅓ inch thick. Place the slices on unlined cookie sheets and bake until dry to the touch, about 20 minutes. Cool on cookie sheets.
- Melt chocolate chips and drizzle over cookies, if desired.
- Store in an airtight container for up to 3 days, or freeze for up to 3 months.

orange stir 'n' drop

dairy-free

yield: 4 dozen cookies

A recipe so simple it's the perfect first step for kids to start baking on their own. Stamping the cookies with a glass is a task even the tiniest hands can accomplish.

2 large eggs, at room temperature

⅔ cup vegetable oil

1 tablespoon vanilla extract

1 teaspoon freshly grated orange zest

¾ cup granulated sugar

2 cups all-purpose flour

2 teaspoons baking powder

½ teaspoon salt

Orange decorating sugar

- Preheat the oven to 375°F. Line 2 cookie sheets with parchment paper.
- Place the eggs, oil, vanilla, and orange zest in a large mixer bowl and beat until well combined. Add the sugar and beat until thickened. With the mixer on low, stir in the flour, baking powder, and salt until well combined.
- Using a level small (2 teaspoon size) cookie scoop, drop the batter about 2 inches apart on the prepared cookie sheets.
- Stamp each cookie flat with the bottom of a glass dipped in decorating sugar. (Lightly oil the glass, then dip in sugar. Repeat dipping in sugar so bottom of glass is completely covered each time.)
- Transfer to the oven and bake until the edges of the cookies are lightly browned, 8 to 10 minutes, rotating the cookie sheets on the oven racks halfway through the baking time. Cool on the cookie sheets for 3 minutes. Transfer to wire racks and cool completely. Repeat with the remaining dough on cool cookie sheets.
- Store in an airtight container for up to 3 days, or freeze for up to 3 months.

flourless oatmeal raisin cookies

gluten-free

yield: about 2½ dozen cookies

Marcia Lemberg has been an ardent Cookies for Kids' Cancer supporter for years. She has baked for and worked at dozens and dozens of bake sales, where she gets requests for gluten-free cookies all the time. She found a recipe online, made some changes, and came up with these yummy drop cookies. They sell out every time.

4 packets (1.51 ounces each) maple and brown sugar instant oatmeal (we used Quaker)

¼ cup granulated sugar

¼ cup light brown sugar

1 large egg, at room temperature

⅓ cup canola oil

1 tablespoon vanilla extract

1 cup of either raisins, cranberries, Raisinets, chocolate chips, or nuts

- Place the contents of the 4 packets of oatmeal in a large bowl. Stir in the sugars. Stir in remaining ingredients. Mix until well combined. Cover and refrigerate 30 minutes.

- Preheat the oven to 350°F. Line 2 cookie sheets with parchment paper.

- Form the dough into teaspoon-size balls and place them 2 inches apart on the prepared cookie sheets.

- Transfer to the oven and bake until the cookies begin to brown at the edges, 11 to 13 minutes, rotating the cookie sheets on the oven racks halfway through the baking time. Cool on the cookie sheets for 3 minutes. Transfer to wire racks to cool completely. Repeat with the remaining dough on cool cookie sheets.

- Store in an airtight container for up to 3 days, or freeze for up to 3 months.

rice flour wafers

gluten-free

yield: about 3 dozen wafers

Rice is often a go-to for gluten-free cooking, and this cookie takes advantage of rice flour's ability to be a stand-in for wheat. The cookies are simple, but the sprinkles really dress them up.

4 large egg whites, at room temperature

½ cup granulated sugar

1½ cups brown rice flour, sifted

1 stick (¼ pound) unsalted butter, at room temperature

1 teaspoon vanilla extract

½ teaspoon almond extract

Decorating sugar or gluten-free sprinkles (optional)

- Preheat the oven to 350°F. Line 2 cookie sheets with parchment paper.
- Place the egg whites in a large mixer bowl and beat until foamy. Add the sugar and beat until blended. Stir in the rice flour and mix to combine. Fold the butter and vanilla and almond extracts into the flour mixture.
- Using a heaping small (2-teaspoon size) cookie scoop, drop the dough about 2 inches apart on the prepared cookie sheets. Spread thin with the back of a rice-floured spoon. Top with decorating sugar or sprinkles, if using.
- Transfer to the oven and bake until the cookies just begin to brown on the edges, 12 minutes, rotating the cookie sheets on the oven racks halfway through the baking time. Cool on the cookie sheets 5 minutes. Transfer to wire racks to cool completely. Repeat with the remaining dough on cool cookie sheets.
- Store in an airtight container for up to 3 days, or freeze for up to 3 months.

doggie cookies

yield: about 3 dozen 3-inch cookies

When we said everyone can have a cookie, we meant everyone, even your pups. Don't worry if a kid gets hold of one: They're made with real food.

One 6-ounce jar turkey, rice and vegetable puréed baby food

1 large egg, at room temperature, beaten

1 tablespoon vegetable oil

1¼ cups brown rice flour, plus more for rolling

½ cup old-fashioned or quick-cooking oats

- Preheat the oven to 325°F. Line 2 cookie sheets with parchment paper.

- Place baby food, egg, and oil in a large bowl and beat with a fork until well combined. Stir in flour and oats and mix together.

- Roll half the dough out onto a floured surface to ⅛-inch thickness. If the dough is too sticky, add more flour. Using a cookie cutter, cut out shapes and transfer to the prepared cookie sheets. Repeat with remaining dough.

- Transfer to the oven and bake 30 minutes. Turn the oven off and leave cookies in the oven to crisp up for 15 minutes. Transfer the cookies to a wire rack and cool completely.

- **baker's note** These cookies can easily be made by using a heaping small (2-teaspoon size) cookie scoop to drop the dough about 1 inch apart on the prepared cookie sheets. Press down with a spatula to flatten.

- Store in an airtight container for up to 3 days, or freeze for up to 3 months.

Birmingham, AL

CINDY HATCHER
Birmingham, AL

In the world of food magazines, we're often thinking about what good food can mean to our audience. It has the power to energize, to warm bellies and hearts, to restore faith in your ability to make something yummy, and to provide comfort for you and your family. This is the same power that Gretchen and the good folks at Cookies for Kids' Cancer have bestowed on the almighty cookie, and with great success: Their bake sales have raised millions to help fund pediatric cancer research—one powerful, tasty cookie at a time.

My colleagues at *Cooking Light*—along with coworkers at our sister publications of *Southern Living*, *Coastal Living*, and *Oxmoor House*—were familiar with Gretchen's story and decided it was time to do our part, combining our love of food with our heartfelt support of Cookies for Kids' Cancer. So we came together to hold our own Birmingham, Alabama, bake sale. It was a gorgeous September football Saturday in the South—a fact that should've doomed us to thumb-twiddlingly scarce crowds—yet we placed hundreds of cookies in the hands of people who were eager to hear about the cause. By the end of the market, we were astonished to learn that we would be adding about $1,000 to the Cookies for Kids' Cancer jar.

It came down to the little details that had the biggest positive impact on our sale: extra care labeling and packaging cookies that turned some of them into miniature works of art; a genius idea to make a competition between our state's two rival football teams to see which side could sell the most cookies in their team's colors; a cookie-decorating booth that forced parents to stop and listen to our message while their child gleefully iced and sprinkled and glittered.

"It was heartwarming to see how the staff came together for our bake sale—everyone wanted to help," says Ann Pittman, *Cooking Light*'s executive food editor. "If they couldn't be at the actual sale, they cheerily baked dozens of their favorite cookies, or spent time making signs or packaging cute cookie parcels. We all wanted to be part of the bake sale action!"

celebrate

cookie press hearts

yield: about 10 dozen cookies

Remember what we said about cookies being made with love? This one really is: First of all, it's a heart. And then there's the pink crystal sugar.

3 sticks (¾ pound) unsalted butter, at room temperature

1 cup granulated sugar

½ teaspoon salt

2 large eggs, at room temperature

1 tablespoon vanilla extract

3⅓ cups all-purpose flour

Decorating sugar (any color)

- Preheat the oven to 400°F. Line 2 cookie sheets with parchment paper.

- Place the butter, sugar, and salt in a large mixer bowl. Beat until smooth and creamy, about 3 minutes. Add the eggs one at a time, beating after each addition, and the vanilla.

- Slowly add flour, beating until well incorporated. Scrape down the sides of the bowl and mix again.

- Spoon dough into cookie press fitted with heart template. Squeeze dough onto the prepared cookie sheets 1 to 2 inches apart. Sprinkle with decorating sugar. Using the palm of your hand, gently press down.

- Transfer to the oven and bake until the cookies begin to brown slightly at the edges, 8 to 10 minutes, rotating the cookie sheets on the oven racks halfway through the baking time. Cool on the cookie sheets for 3 minutes. Transfer to wire racks to cool completely. Repeat with the remaining dough on cool cookie sheets.

- Store in an airtight container for up to 3 days, or freeze for up to 3 months.

surefire gingerbread cookies

yield: about 6 dozen cookies.

Hannah Kluger's mom has been making these for years. Hannah's now baking them with her kids and doesn't consider Christmas complete unless there's a batch within easy reach during the entire holiday season for everyone in the family.

2 sticks (½ pound) unsalted butter, at room temperature

¼ cup water

½ cup light brown sugar

½ cup molasses

3 cups all-purpose flour

1 teaspoon baking soda

1 teaspoon salt

1½ teaspoons ground ginger

½ teaspoon ground cinnamon

½ teaspoon ground nutmeg

⅛ teaspoon ground cloves

Dried currants or candies for decorating (optional)

Royal icing for decorating (optional, see page 42)

- Place the butter and water in a large glass bowl and place in microwave. Microwave on high for 1 minute or until butter is melted. Add the sugar and molasses and stir until smooth.

- Place the flour, baking soda, salt, ginger, cinnamon, nutmeg, and cloves in a separate bowl; mix well and gradually add to the butter mixture, stirring with a wooden spoon. Stir until all flour is incorporated, using your hands to work all of the flour in if dough becomes too stiff to stir.

- Divide the dough in half; shape each half into a disk; and wrap in plastic wrap. Refrigerate for at least 8 hours and up to 3 days.

- Preheat the oven to 350°F. Line 2 cookie sheets with parchment paper.

- On a lightly floured surface, use a lightly floured rolling pin to roll the dough ⅛ inch thick. Cut with 2½-inch cookie cutters and place 1 inch apart on the prepared cookie sheets. Decorate with currants or candies now, if using. Transfer to the oven and bake for 8 to 11 minutes, rotating the cookie sheets on the oven racks halfway through the baking time.

Cool on the cookie sheets for 3 minutes. Transfer to wire racks to cool completely. Repeat with the remaining dough on cool cookie sheets.

- If decorating with royal icing, decorate after cookies are completely cool.

- Store in an airtight container for up to 3 days, or freeze for up to 3 months.

spread the word ❀ Get Macaroni Kid involved. Most communities have a local Macaroni Kid Newsletter that spreads the word about family-friendly events. As supporters of Cookies for Kids' Cancer, Macaroni Kid Publishers are happy to spread the word and will often get involved.

cute counts ❀ Add a Cookies logo sticker to a sand pail, bucket, or any clear container, and you'll have the perfect donation jar.

cranberry-pistachio biscotti

Wearing red and green on the inside, these biscotti are holiday-ready for a bake sale or gift-giving. Like our Mandel Bread, it's a crunchy, sweet cookie with no dairy.

3¾ cups all-purpose flour

2 cups granulated sugar

1 teaspoon baking powder

¼ teaspoon salt

3 large eggs, at room temperature

3 large egg yolks, at room temperature

1 teaspoon vanilla extract

2 tablespoons water

1 cup shelled pistachios

1 cup dried cranberries

- Preheat the oven to 375°F. Line a cookie sheet with parchment paper.

- Place the flour, sugar, baking powder, and salt in a large mixer bowl; mix well.

- Place the eggs, egg yolks, vanilla, and water in a separate bowl; mix well and add to the dry ingredients. Beat until everything is well incorporated. Scrape down the sides of the bowl, add the pistachios and cranberries, and mix again.

- Using floured hands, form the dough into 2 balls and then shape each ball into a 12-inch log. Place logs about 4 inches apart on the prepared cookie sheet. Transfer to the oven and bake until the tops begin to crack, about 20 to 25 minutes. Set aside to cool for 10 minutes.

- Reduce the oven temperature to 325°F. Transfer the baked logs to a cutting board and using a very sharp straight-edged knife, slice the logs on a slight diagonal, about ⅓ inch thick. Place slices on unlined cookie sheets and bake until dry to the touch, about 20 minutes. Cool on cookie sheets.

- Store in an airtight container for up to 3 days, or freeze for up to 3 months.

speculaas

yield: 10 dozen cookies

Quite possibly the single most buttery spice cookie we have ever tasted. It radiates holiday with every whiff that floats out of the oven as they bake. After baking 3,840 cookies, we think this is our fave.

2 sticks (½ pound) unsalted butter, at room temperature

1 cup light brown sugar

2½ cups all-purpose flour

¼ teaspoon baking soda

¼ teaspoon salt

2 teaspoons ground cinnamon

1 teaspoon ground nutmeg

¼ teaspoon ground cloves

⅓ cup plain yogurt

1½ cups sliced almonds

- Place the butter and sugar in a large mixer bowl and beat until smooth and creamy, about 3 minutes. Place the flour, baking soda, salt, cinnamon, nutmeg, and cloves in a separate bowl; mix well. Add one-third of the flour mixture and beat, then add half of the yogurt and beat. Continue alternating flour with yogurt, finishing with flour. Scrape down the sides of the bowl. Add the nuts and mix again.

- Line an 8 x 8-inch baking pan with plastic wrap. Press the dough into the pan and cover with plastic wrap; use your palm or a measuring cup to smooth the top. Refrigerate for at least 8 hours and up to 3 days.

- Preheat the oven to 350°F. Line 2 cookie sheets with parchment paper.

- Remove the dough from the pan and cut into 3 equal pieces. Slice dough in ⅛-inch slices and place ½ inch apart on the prepared cookie sheets.

- Transfer to the oven and bake until the cookies begin to brown at the edges, 8 to 10 minutes, rotating the cookie sheets on the oven racks halfway through the baking time. Cool on the cookie sheets for 3 minutes. Transfer to wire racks to cool completely. Repeat with the remaining dough on cool cookie sheets.

- Store in an airtight container for up to 3 days, or freeze for up to 3 months.

benne burgers

yield: 6 dozen filled cookies

Nutty-tasting sesame seeds are called "benne" in the South. With their luscious chocolate ganache filling, these sandwich cookies resemble burgers in sesame buns.

One 7-ounce tube almond paste

¾ cup granulated sugar

2 tablespoons cornstarch

Pinch salt

2 large egg whites, at room temperature

¼ teaspoon vanilla extract

1 cup sesame seeds

1 cup sour cream ganache (see page 53)

- Break the almond paste into pieces and place in the bowl of a food processor with sugar, cornstarch, and salt. Process until well combined. Add the egg whites and vanilla and process again. The mixture will be fairly smooth and shiny. Refrigerate for 1 hour or up to 3 days.

- Preheat the oven to 350°F. Line 2 cookie sheets with parchment paper.

- Scoop level small (2-teaspoon size) cookie scoops of batter into the sesame seeds and coat completely. Place 1½ inches apart on the prepared cookie sheets and bake 13 to 15 minutes, rotating the cookie sheets on the oven racks halfway through the baking time. Cool on the cookie sheets for 3 minutes. Transfer to wire racks to cool completely. Repeat with the remaining batter on cool cookie sheets.

- **To fill cookies:** Place ganache in a freezer-weight resealable bag, then snip off a corner. Pipe 1 teaspoon of ganache on 1 cookie and top with another.

- Store filled cookies in the refrigerator for up to 3 days. Do not freeze.

Aurora, OH

TERRI KRAFCIK
Aurora, OH

- - - - - - - - - - - - - - - - - - - -

A little over 4 years ago my daughter Mackenzie, now 7½, mentioned to me that she wanted to help raise money for sick children.

Just a few weeks later, I read about Cookies for Kids' Cancer in *Food & Wine* magazine. When I went to the website, I was amazed by the story of a little boy named Liam who was fighting cancer at the age of four. His situation was heartbreaking, and I remember thinking, "This is a great cause!" We'd host a bake sale, and even if we only raised $100, what an incredible way to teach my daughter that anyone, at any age, can make a difference.

Every tool you could possibly need to host a bake sale is on the Cookies for Kids' Cancer website. Never having attempted anything like this before, I realized I had nothing to lose, only everything to gain. Little did I know how rewarding this experience would be in so many ways!

We held our first annual Cookies for Kids' Cancer Bake Sale in December 2008. I e-mailed about 20 neighbors and friends to ask if they would be willing to bake. Given that we live in Ohio, we needed to be somewhere inside—outside in December wouldn't work. Hoping to catch plenty of foot traffic, we decided to hold our sale at the elementary school during basketball games, when approximately 800 to 900 people would be there. We raised $60 before we had even finished setting up. As the day progressed, I knew this would be an annual thing for us and brainstormed ideas for the following year. I remember looking at my daughter after hour 8 of the sale and telling her it was time to go. She replied, "Already?" I was thrilled when I counted up $800. This past December we held our fourth sale and raised over $1,150 with the sweet contributions of 37 bakers, most having been involved since the start. Mackenzie and I are already looking ahead to our next sale.

KATE LUBENESKY/SHEILA GIBBONS
Montclair, NJ

The Van Vleck Gardens Bake Sale was held on the Saturday before Mother's Day in Montclair, New Jersey. The Van Vleck is a gorgeous house and garden turned into a museum that was built in the late 1800s. The Chinese wisteria planted in the '30s that wraps around the courtyard garden is stunning. Having a bake sale on the same day as their garden sale was perfect timing for a big crowd. The day was lovely and the crowd was generous. With a matching donation from a local business, we raised over $6,000, but the most moving moment came as we were wrapping up for the day. A man came up and told us that 16 years ago he lost his son to cancer. Without taking a single cookie, he simply slipped $50 into our jar. It was heartbreaking and beautiful and the reason we will host another event.

KATHY McBRIDE
Staten Island, NY

The first year, it was 104 degrees when the inaugural McBride Cup Roller Hockey game benefiting Cookies for Kids' Cancer was played. The second year, it was snowing and in the 30s.

The troublesome weather cut attendance but didn't stop a hardy group of roller hockey fans from braving slushy roads and falling branches to get to Staten Island Roller Hockey in Castleton Corners for this year's Cup game, which pitted the Staten Island Advance team against Pack Hockey.

The game was played in honor of Sean McBride, a longtime Staten Island Advance employee who died in October 2009 at the age of 42.

He was a huge New York Rangers fan and passed on his love of hockey to our sons Brian, Patrick, and Connor.

Patrick, 18, and Brian, 16, are also roller hockey enthusiasts and were numbers 25 and 10 on the Advance side. They and their younger brother, Connor, 13, play in leagues at the Roller Hockey rink.

At the Cup, cookies, chocolate-covered pretzels, hot beverages, and other goodies were sold, and raffles were offered with 100% of proceeds going to benefit Cookies for Kids' Cancer in Sean's name. We raised over $1,000.

The first year brought heat. The second year brought snow. We're excited to see what this year will bring.

prune hamantashalas

yield: about 5 dozen cookies

Purim, a holiday that celebrates the good Queen Esther saving the Jewish people of Persia from the evils of Prime Minister Haman, is the only Jewish holiday that has a cookie associated with it. He wore a tricorner hat, mimicked in these traditional cookies. Ours are called "Hamantashalas" because they're little.

for prune filling

1 heaping cup pitted prunes, firmly packed (one 9-ounce package)

Boiling water

1 tablespoon fresh lemon juice

1 teaspoon freshly grated lemon zest

for cookie dough

2 large eggs, at room temperature

½ cup granulated sugar

¼ cup canola oil

1 tablespoon fresh lemon juice

2 teaspoons freshly grated lemon zest

1 teaspoon vanilla extract

2½ cups all-purpose flour

1 teaspoon baking powder

- Preheat the oven to 350°F. Line 2 cookie sheets with parchment paper.

- **To make the prune filling:** Place prunes in a medium bowl and cover with boiling water. Set aside for 15 minutes. Drain the prunes, place in food processor fitted with metal blade and purée. Add lemon juice and zest and pulse to blend. Scrape down the sides of the bowl and blend again.

- **To make the cookie dough:** Place the eggs and sugar in a mixer bowl and beat until well combined. Add the oil, lemon juice, lemon zest, and vanilla and beat until well combined. Place the flour and baking powder in a separate bowl, mix well, and add to the egg mixture. Stir until well combined.

prune hamantashalas (cont.)

- Divide the dough into 3 pieces and shape each into a disk. On a lightly floured surface, roll the dough out to ⅛ inch thick. Cut circles with a 2½-inch round cookie cutter.

- Place a heaping small (2-teaspoon size) cookie scoop of prune filling in the center of each circle, then fold up sides and pinch the corners to form a triangle shape. Place on the prepared cookie sheets, about 1 inch apart, and bake until golden, 20 to 30 minutes, rotating the cookie sheets on the oven racks halfway through the baking time. Cool on the cookie sheets for 3 minutes. Transfer to wire racks to cool completely. Repeat with the remaining dough and filling on cool cookie sheets.

- Store in an airtight container for up to 3 days, or freeze for up to 3 months.

baked goods with "buzz" � Offer treats from local "celebrities." Sports figures or local newscasters or even the mayor could be an added draw to bring in big donations and extra supporters. Highlight their treats on the table as a way to generate excitement and encourage higher donations for treats with name recognition.

cute counts ✻ Use balloons! This is a simple way to "spruce up" your table/tent.

cheesecake slices

Two passions in one: cheesecake in a cookie, with a circle of graham cracker "crust." Inspired by a cookie from our friends in the *Better Homes and Gardens* test kitchen, it's packed with flavor.

1½ sticks (6 ounces) unsalted butter, at room temperature	2 tablespoons fresh lemon juice
4 ounces cream cheese	1½ teaspoons vanilla extract
¾ cup granulated sugar	2¼ cups all-purpose flour
2 teaspoons freshly grated lemon zest	3 graham crackers, finely crushed (⅓ cup)
2 teaspoons freshly grated orange zest	

- Place the butter and cream cheese in a large mixer bowl and beat until smooth and creamy, about 30 seconds. Add the sugar, lemon zest, orange zest, lemon juice and vanilla, one at a time, beating after each addition. Beat well and scrape down the sides of the bowl. With the mixer on low, add the flour and mix until well incorporated.

- Divide the dough in half, form each piece into a 10-inch log, and then roll in graham cracker crumbs. Cover each log and refrigerate for at least 3 hours and up to 3 days.

- Preheat the oven to 375°F. Line 2 cookie sheets with parchment paper.

- With a serrated knife, cut the logs into ¼-inch slices. Place 1 inch apart on the prepared cookie sheets and bake until the bottoms are lightly browned, 8 to 10 minutes, rotating the cookie sheets on the oven racks halfway through the baking time. Cool on the cookie sheets for 3 minutes. Transfer to wire racks to cool completely. Repeat with the remaining dough on cool cookie sheets.

- Store in an airtight container for up to 3 days, or freeze for up to 3 months.

apricot & raspberry thumbprints

yield: about 2½ dozen cookies

We like the contrast of apricot and raspberry in our thumbprints, but any preserve you choose will work. You can use jam, jelly, or pure fruit spreads too.

1 stick (¼ pound) unsalted butter, at room temperature

¾ cup confectioners' sugar, plus 2 teaspoons for dusting

1 large egg, at room temperature

1 teaspoon vanilla extract

1¾ cups all-purpose flour

¼ teaspoon salt

3 tablespoons apricot preserves

3 tablespoons seedless red raspberry preserves

- Place the butter, ¾ cup confectioners' sugar, egg, and vanilla in a large mixer bowl and beat until smooth and creamy, about 3 minutes. Scrape down the sides of the bowl. With the mixer on low, add flour and salt, beat well, and scrape again.

- Divide the dough in half; shape each into a disk, and wrap separately in plastic. Chill until firm, about 1 hour.

- Preheat the oven to 375°F. Line 2 cookie sheets with parchment paper.

- Using a level small (2-teaspoon size) cookie scoop, drop the dough 2 inches apart on the prepared cookie sheets. Using your thumb, gently press in the center of the dough. Transfer to the oven and bake until the edges are lightly browned, 8 to 10 minutes, rotating the cookie sheets on the oven racks halfway through the baking time. Cool the cookies on the cookie sheets for 3 minutes. Transfer to the wire racks and cool completely. Repeat with the remaining dough on cool cookie sheets.

- Fill each center of half of the cookies with ½ teaspoon of apricot preserves. Fill remaining cookies with raspberry preserves. Dust the cookies with the remaining 2 teaspoons confectioners' sugar.

- Store in an airtight container for up to 3 days, or freeze for up to 3 months.

New York, NY

L'ORÉAL USA
Kentucky, Ohio, New Jersey,
New York, Texas

In the Corporate Communications Office we are always looking for interesting ways to engage our employees and to give back. At a brainstorming meeting with our colleagues in PR, we asked if any of their brands had a cause that we could help galvanize our employees around. Nashelly Messina, who helps to organize the Women of Worth program for L'Oréal Paris, piped up and started talking about Gretchen, a L'Oréal Paris Women of Worth Honoree, and her incredible nonprofit, Cookies for Kids' Cancer.

The idea was simply perfect and easy to execute. We casually sent an email out to our facilities across the country to tell them about this bake sale we planned to host in New York and the children that would benefit from the money we raised, and almost immediately nearly every facility signed up to participate.

On Valentine's Day, eleven

L'Oréal USA facilities across the country came together to raise $16,000 for pediatric cancer research. Employees baked over 3,000 cookies and volunteered to help plan and facilitate this grassroots effort. The response from employees was incredible. In fact, we received notes telling us how much it meant to our employees to support Cookies for Kids' Cancer and how they felt like they were really making a difference.

The L'Oréal USA team is passionate about giving back and helping others, and this particular cause touched all our hearts. The events were so successful and loved that this bigger-than-life bake sale will take place again in 2013. The L'Oréal USA group is committed to helping make the letter "C" stand for "Cookies"!

BOSTON FOOD SWAP
Boston, MA

The Boston Cookie Swap festivities started at 2 p.m., when Santa greeted attendees downstairs at Space with a Soul and directed them to the seventh-floor loft, which we'd decorated with gold tablecloths and a holiday-themed photo booth.

After checking in and sharing the number of cookies they'd brought, swappers found a spot for displaying their goodies. In addition to sampling cookies, swappers enjoyed sampling holiday flavors of seltzer, creating clothespin reindeer in the craft corner, and posing in the photo booth.

Around 3 p.m., Melissa from Swap.com made announcements and we handed out GladWare, which the swappers and snackers filled with cookies. With dozens of cookies to choose from, including Cappuccino "Kisses," Goat Cheese and Lime Cheesecake Thumbprints, Reindeer Pinwheels, and Peppermint Meringues, it was tough to choose a favorite. In the end, we crowned two winners in our cookie contest: Jared Lazzaro for Nonna Bea's Raspberry Squares and Dawn Durkee for her Walnut Shortbread Cookies.

The Raspberry Squares were unfortunately devoured before I could sample them, but Dawn's shortbread was pretty amazing and she even brought some wrapping paper and boxes to create a multi-level display (a swapper after our own hearts!). You can find all the recipes on the Cookie Swap microsite, which was created by our pals at MyReci, a super-cool new platform for organizing recipes online.

All told, we raised $1,000 for Cookies for Kids' Cancer and had a fantastic time in the process. Big thanks to our "swap sisters" Melissa and Amy from Swap.com, as well as Glad to Give, MyReci, KO Catering and Pies, OXO kitchen tools, Udi's Gluten-Free Foods, Space with a Soul, and of course, all our fabulous swappers and snackers.

FAMILY ALLIANCE WITH SUPPORT FROM HUDSON COUNTY OXONIANS
Hoboken, NJ

OXOnians (what we call ourselves at OXO) pulled together to raise almost $10,000 in one day at the Hoboken Arts & Music Festival. We spent a few late nights in the OXO test kitchen baking cookies, which were subsequently transported across the Hudson River. Local Hoboken favorites such as Carlo's Bake Shop (home of the Cake Boss), Giorgio's, Old German Bakery, Gammarrerl's, and Ultramarino's generously donated baked goods. P9, a design firm located in Hudson County, donated $5,000 along with some delicious cookies. The Hoboken Family Alliance donated the cost of the booth location and tent rental.

Our OXO team literally lost their voices corralling people into our booth, which was packed with hungry festivalgoers. You know what they say in real estate. Location. Location. Location.

blimey limey cookies

yield: about 3½ dozen cookies

Ah, St. Paddy's Day—the perfect holiday because everyone can celebrate, Irish or not. We choose to honor it with cookies, of course: a tender lime shamrock with a coat of shiny green.

2 sticks (½ pound) unsalted butter, at room temperature

¾ cup granulated sugar

¼ cup fresh lime juice

2 teaspoons freshly grated lime zest

1 teaspoon vanilla extract

2½ cups all-purpose flour

1 cup ground almonds

Green decorating sugar

- Preheat the oven to 350°F. Line 2 cookie sheets with parchment paper.

- Place the butter and sugar in a large mixer bowl and beat until smooth and creamy, about 3 minutes. Add the lime juice, lime zest, and vanilla, beating to combine. Scrape down the sides of the bowl and beat again. With the mixer on low, add flour and beat, scraping again, until combined. Stir in almonds and mix until well combined.

- Divide the dough into 3 disks. Place the disks between 2 well-floured sheets of waxed paper and roll out to a scant ¼-inch thickness (sprinkle with additional flour if dough is sticky). Using a 2½ inch shamrock cookie cutter, cut out shapes and place on the prepared cookie sheets, about 2 inches apart. Sprinkle tops of shamrocks with decorating sugar.

- Transfer to the oven and bake until the cookies just begin to brown on the edges, 10 to 12 minutes, rotating the cookie sheets on the oven racks halfway through the baking time. Cool on the cookie sheets for 3 minutes. Transfer to wire racks and cool completely. Repeat with the remaining dough on cool cookie sheets.

- Store in an airtight container for up to 3 days, or freeze for up to 3 months.

mother's day chocolate-coconut triangles

yield: 2 dozen cookie triangles

Cindy Grell organized a town-wide bake sale in her hometown of Cranford, New Jersey in honor of Liam's birthday. These gooey and sweet triangular bars, with a double dose of chocolate intensity from the cookie crust and a bittersweet chip layer, are one of her faves.

One 9-ounce package chocolate crisp wafer cookies (Nabisco Famous wafers)

¾ stick (6 tablespoons) unsalted butter, melted

1 teaspoon vanilla extract

One 14-ounce can sweetened condensed milk

3 large egg whites, at room temperature

One 14-ounce bag sweetened flaked coconut

2 cups (12 ounces) bittersweet chocolate chips

- Preheat the oven to 350°F. Line a 9 x 13-inch baking pan with foil.
- Place the wafer cookies in a food processor fitted with a steel blade and process until fine crumbs. Add the melted butter and vanilla and pulse until evenly distributed. Press the crumbs into the bottom of the prepared pan. Transfer to the oven and bake for 8 minutes.
- Meanwhile, place the condensed milk and egg whites in a bowl and whisk until well combined. Stir in coconut.
- Remove the pan from the oven and sprinkle crust evenly with chocolate chips. Spoon the coconut mixture on top. Spread evenly with a fork to keep the rough texture. Return pan to the oven and bake until top is set and golden, 30 to 35 minutes.
- Transfer the pan to a wire rack to cool completely. Lift the parchment paper by the ends onto cutting board. Cut into 12 squares; cut each square into 2 triangles.
- Store in an airtight container for up to 3 days, or freeze for up to 3 months.

pumpkin whoopie pies

yield: about 3½ dozen cookies

Pumpkin pie might have met its match here: all the familiar sweetness and spice in a two-bite treat you can eat without a fork. Bake cookies the day before your bake sale, then fill to order or just before packing.

for the cookies

1½ sticks (6 ounces) unsalted butter, at room temperature

1 cup granulated sugar

½ cup light brown sugar

3 large eggs, at room temperature

One 15-ounce can pumpkin purée

2 teaspoons vanilla extract

3 cups all-purpose flour

1 tablespoon ground pumpkin pie spice

1½ teaspoons baking powder

1 teaspoon baking soda

1 teaspoon ground cinnamon

½ teaspoon salt

for the filling

One 7½-ounce jar marshmallow creme (Fluff)

4 ounces cream cheese, at room temperature

- Preheat the oven to 350°F. Line 2 cookie sheets with parchment paper.
- **To make cookies:** Place the butter and sugars in a large mixer bowl and beat until smooth and creamy, about 3 minutes. Add the eggs one at a time, beating after each addition. Add the pumpkin and vanilla and beat well. Scrape down the sides of the bowl and beat again. Place the flour, pumpkin pie spice, baking powder, baking soda, cinnamon, and salt in a separate bowl and mix to combine. With the mixer on low, add to the pumpkin mixture and mix until well combined.
- Using a level small (2-teaspoon size) cookie scoop, drop the dough about 2 inches apart on the prepared cookie sheets.
- Transfer to the oven and bake just until the edges of the cookies are lightly browned, 10 to 12 minutes, rotating the cookie sheets on the oven

racks halfway through the baking time. Cool on the cookie sheets for 3 minutes. Transfer to wire racks and cool completely. Repeat with the remaining dough on cool cookie sheets.

- **To make the filling:** Place the marshmallow creme and cream cheese in a bowl and beat until fluffy, about 3 minutes. Spread a teaspoonful of filling onto the flat side of half of the cookies. Top with remaining cookies. Gently squeeze cookie sandwiches so filling spreads to the edge.
- Store filled cookies in the refrigerator for up to 1 day. Do not freeze.

spread the word ❀ Make sure the PTA committees at school know about the upcoming sale. Middle and high school kids often belong to clubs that include earning credit for community work.

be prepared ❀ For hot (or even warm) days, have a cooler for storing extra baked goods that you don't have room to display on your table.

cute counts ❀ Cut the sides from cardboard boxes and use them to make signs for your event. They'll go great with your kraft paper tablecloths!

peppermint meringues

yield: about 4 dozen cookies

Starlight mints add a jewel-like shimmer to these crisp stars. No flour or dairy means this treat is good for just about everyone.

¾ cup confectioners' sugar

½ cup (3 ounces) finely crushed peppermint candy

3 large egg whites, at room temperature

½ teaspoon fresh lemon juice

¼ teaspoon salt

½ cup granulated sugar

- Preheat the oven to 200°F. Line 2 cookie sheets with parchment paper.
- Place the confectioners' sugar and peppermint candy in a medium bowl and mix to combine.
- Place the egg whites, lemon juice, and salt in the bowl of a mixer fitted with a whisk and beat until foamy. Add granulated sugar, 1 tablespoon at a time. Increase the speed to high and beat until stiff peaks form. Gently fold the confectioners' sugar mixture into the egg whites until no white streaks remain.
- Fill a disposable pastry bag fitted with a large star tip and pipe about 1 tablespoon of the batter, 1 inch apart, on the prepared cookie sheets, or drop the batter by level tablespoons.
- Transfer to the oven and bake for 1 hour. Turn the oven off and leave the meringues in the oven for at least an additional hour.
- Store in an airtight container for up to 3 days, or freeze for up to 3 months.

get organized ❄ Organize volunteers with ease by using on-line sites like Volunteer Spot, Patch.com, or Sign-Up Genius to get friends and family involved.

Santa Cruz, CA

CARA PEARSON/MICHELLE RIDDLE
Santa Cruz, CA

The inaugural Mama's Night Out was held in May to coincide with the birth month of cancer warrior Liam Witt, who inspired Cookies for Kids' Cancer. As co-chairs, we were determined to turn our grief over Liam losing his battle—at just six years old—into action.

The event was everything we had hoped for and more. Our goal was 200 mamas, but we would have been happy with 100. In the end, we had 275! To see all these women come out to support a cause that had become so important to us was overwhelming.

Even more wonderful was the fact that when I told Liam's mom, Gretchen, our plan, she said she would come. We didn't get our hopes up, because we knew that May was going to be a busy month for her, and cross-country travel from New York to California might not be in the cards. But to our joy,

a few days before the event, a Facebook update from Gretchen confirmed that she really was making the trip.

As things got crazy those last few days, it was easy to just stop and think of Gretchen walking in and seeing over 250 women there to support her cause and know that all the work was worth it. As we watched everyone streaming in, we kept looking for Gretchen. Suddenly, the doors opened, and there she was. Cara and I tried not to cry, but it was impossible. How could we not? Later that night, Gretchen said to the crowd, "Liam loved a party, and he would have loved this one." We raised over $20,000.

Lebanon, NJ

TRACY HORNBY
Rutgers University, NJ

Team Cookies for Kids' Cancer made its debut at the Rutgers UNITE Half Marathon in New Jersey. Running in bright orange T-shirts with the Cookies logo and marked in memory of Prince Liam the Brave, 25 runners and walkers (cheered by 55 volunteers!) took over the streets of New Brunswick.

Led by co-chairs Tracy Hornby and Mary Paulson, friends and colleagues at Morris Hills High School in Rockaway, team members raised over $11,000 the first year. The group included Tracy's dad, Rick Kepniss, who walked his first half marathon at age 62! Volunteers included students from service and honor societies at Morris Hills High School, members of Girl Scout Brownie Troop 80382, and members of the surrounding Clinton Township community. Everyone was so pumped that immediately after crossing the finish line, the conversation turned to "next year." We hadn't even driven off the Rutgers campus yet!

Team Cookies for Kids' Cancer blossomed from the start. We almost doubled the amount of runners and walkers simply by telling people about the Cookies mission and letting them know that crossing that finish line, no matter how long it takes to get there, means more than words could ever say to the children and families afflicted by pediatric cancer. Cookies for Kids' Cancer isn't just about selling cookies, it's about being a "Good Cookie" and doing the right thing on behalf of these precious and innocent children. Running, walking, volunteering—no matter what role you play on our team, you're a "Good Cookie"!

KRIS SCHEPPLER
Ames, IA

Our event was held on a Saturday in December at a grocery store in Ames, Iowa. My husband and daughter helped me the day of the sale. I ask friends and members of my church to help by contributing baked goods. I also baked for 3 straight days prior to the sale. I mostly made cookies from the Cookies cookbook. I also made my homemade butter crunch! My little friend Eli Horn got out of the hospital on "leave" for a few hours and came to my house to help me decorate sugar cookies.

I'm not sure how many people came by our bake sale booth on the day of the sale, but we made nearly $900. We did a free-will donation and it was awesome!!! People gave so generously. I used all of the bags, twist ties, and stickers from the bake sale kit I ordered to decorate!

P.S. The day Eli came to help me decorate cookies was the last time I saw him. He left the next day for New York City for his bone marrow transplant and passed away 6 weeks later.

pecan not diamonds

yield: 6 dozen squares

Ultra-rich and loaded with nuts sitting on a buttery short crust, this classic treat is typically cut in a diamond shape. Lovely, but too much waste: We cut squares so every one is a perfect bite.

for the crust

1 stick (¼ pound) unsalted butter, at room temperature

⅓ cup granulated sugar

2 cups all-purpose flour

½ teaspoon baking powder

¼ teaspoon salt

for the filling

2½ sticks (10 ounces) unsalted butter

⅔ cup honey

⅓ cup granulated sugar

1⅓ cups light brown sugar

6 cups pecans

⅓ cup heavy or whipping cream

1 tablespoon vanilla extract

- Preheat the oven to 350 F. Line a 9 x 13-inch baking pan with foil.
- **To make the crust:** Place the butter and sugar in a mixer bowl and beat until smooth and creamy, about 3 minutes. Place the flour, baking powder, and salt in a separate bowl; mix well and add to the butter mixture. Beat until everything is well incorporated. Press the dough into the bottom of the foil-lined pan.
- **To make the filling:** Place the butter, honey, and sugars in a large saucepan. Bring to a boil and cook 3 minutes. Stir in pecans, cream, and vanilla.
- Pour the filling over the crust and transfer to the oven. Bake until set and deep brown, 35 to 45 minutes. Cool in the pan on a wire rack. When cool, remove from the pan and cut in 72 pieces.
- Store in an airtight container for up to 3 days, or freeze for up to 3 months.

soft ginger chews

yield: about 5 dozen cookies

Everyone has an opinion on what makes the perfect ginger cookie. This iced drop satisfies all who prefer chewy to crispy.

for the cookies

1 stick (¼ pound) unsalted butter, at room temperature

1 cup light brown sugar

½ cup unsweetened applesauce

1 large egg, at room temperature

1 teaspoon grated fresh ginger

2½ cups all-purpose flour

1 teaspoon baking powder

1 teaspoon ground ginger

½ teaspoon salt

for the icing

½ cup confectioners' sugar

1 tablespoon milk

- Preheat the oven to 350°F. Line 2 cookie sheets with parchment paper.

- **To make the cookies:** Place the butter and brown sugar in a large mixer bowl and beat until smooth and creamy, about 3 minutes. Add the applesauce, egg, and fresh ginger, one at a time, beating after each addition. Scrape down the sides of the bowl. Place the flour, baking powder, ground ginger, and salt in a separate bowl; mix well and add to the butter mixture. Beat until everything is well incorporated.

- Using a heaping small (2-teaspoon size) cookie scoop, drop the dough about 2 inches apart on the prepared cookie sheets.

- Transfer to the oven and bake until the cookies are just beginning to brown on the edges, 8 to 10 minutes, rotating the cookie sheets on the oven racks halfway through the baking time. Cool on the cookie sheets for 3 minutes. Transfer to wire racks and cool completely. Repeat with the remaining dough on cool cookie sheets.

- **To make the icing:** Place confectioners' sugar and milk in a bowl and whisk until well combined. Drizzle icing over cooled cookies.

- Store in an airtight container for up to 3 days, or freeze for up to 3 months.

make it fast

emma's s'mores balls

yield: about 6 dozen cookies

When Emma isn't making hundreds of S'mores Balls to sell at bake sales, she's making beautiful orange bracelets to sell alongside them. The balls are chock-full of s'mores flavors, and Emma says they're great as a frozen treat too.

2 sticks (½ pound) unsalted butter

One 14-ounce can sweetened condensed milk

¼ cup light brown sugar

4 sleeves (19.5 ounces) graham crackers, crushed (or 5 cups purchased crumbs)

2 cups mini marshmallows

2 cups (12 ounces) milk chocolate chips

- Line 2 cookie sheets with waxed paper.
- Place the butter, condensed milk, and brown sugar in a large microwave-safe bowl. Place in microwave and heat until butter is melted. Stir to combine. Add the graham cracker crumbs and stir well to combine. Stir in the marshmallows. Scoop heaping small (2-teaspoon size) cookie scoops of dough; roll into balls and chill.
- Melt the chocolate chips. Dip the bottoms of the balls in melted chocolate, place on waxed paper, and refrigerate for at least 30 minutes.
- Store in the refrigerator for up to 3 days, or freeze for up to 3 months.

spread the word ❀ Ask blogger friends to write a post about your event—this is a great way to share the story of the inspiration behind your event as well as the details for people who would like to attend.

alfajores

yield: 6 dozen cookies

These cookies are popular all over Latin America, and ours are typical of the style from Peru. A super simple piecrust (made in a food processor) is rolled, cut, baked, and then filled with purchased dulce de leche. For a seriously fast version, use refrigerated pie crust.

½ cup sweetened flaked coconut

2½ cups all-purpose flour

¼ cup granulated sugar

½ teaspoon salt

½ cup vegetable shortening

1 stick (¼ pound) unsalted butter, cold

⅓ cup ice water

¾ cup dulce de leche

- Grind the coconut to crumbs in the bowl of a food processor fitted with the metal blade. Cover and set aside.

- Place the flour, sugar, and salt in the bowl of the food processor fitted with the metal blade. Pulse to combine. Add the shortening and pulse to blend with flour mixture until the mixture looks like coarse cornmeal. Cut the cold butter into 1-inch chunks, add to the flour mixture, and pulse 5 to 6 times to distribute butter, leaving it in larger pieces. Add the ice water and pulse 5 to 7 times to bring the dough together. Transfer the dough to a clean surface and shape into a ball. Divide in half, shape each piece into a disk, wrap in plastic, and refrigerate for at least 1 hour and up to 3 days.

- Preheat the oven to 325°F. Line 2 cookie sheets with parchment paper.

- On a floured surface, roll the dough ⅛ inch thick. Cut circles with 1½-inch round fluted cookie cutter and place on the prepared cookie sheets. Transfer to the oven and bake until the cookies begin to brown at the edges, 8 to 10 minutes, rotating the cookie sheets on the oven racks halfway through the baking time. Cool on the cookie sheets for 3 minutes. Transfer to wire racks to cool completely. Repeat with the remaining dough on cool cookie sheets.

- Place ½ teaspoon of dulce de leche on half of the cookies; top with remaining cookies. Gently squeeze the cookie sandwiches so filling spreads to the edge. Roll the edges of the cookies in the ground coconut.
- Store filled cookies in the refrigerator for up to 1 day.
- **baker's note** There's no need to bother cleaning the food processor between grinding the coconut and making the cookie dough.
- **baker's note** To make this recipe in less than 30 minutes, use a package of refrigerated pie crust in place of making the dough from scratch.

---

location, location, location ❀ Want to host an event but can't figure out where? Here are a few ideas:

- Consignment sales
- Farmers market
- Tailgate at a sporting event
- Local pediatrician's office
- School
- Holiday bazaar or festival
- July 4th parade

chocolate-covered peanut butter pretzels

yield: 5 dozen pieces

Chocolate-covered pretzels are huge sellers at bake sales, but they can be a bit time-consuming to make. This version is for those days when you forgot to make something, that "oh darn" moment. And who doesn't like chocolate and peanut butter together?

2 cups (6 ounces) peanut-butter-filled pretzel nuggets

1 cup (6 ounces) semi-sweet chocolate chips

Sprinkles (optional)

- Line a cookie sheet with waxed paper.
- Place the chocolate in a medium microwave-safe bowl and heat in microwave for 1 to 2 minutes, stirring every 30 seconds until completely melted. Stir the peanut butter pretzels into the melted chocolate and coat well. Using a fork, transfer coated pretzels to waxed paper and top with sprinkles, if using.
- Store in the refrigerator for up to 5 days. Do not freeze.

timing counts ❋ Host an event with a theme or around a holiday. From Valentine's Day or St. Patrick's Day to Thanksgiving or the December holidays, let the time of year inspire décor and the treats you offer, and help get supporters to come out and celebrate.

Gilroy, CA

CARMEN MURRAY
Gilroy, GA

My son Ty was diagnosed with stage 4 neuroblastoma at only 16 months old. Though he was only given a 30% chance of surviving for 5 years, he's now a happy, active, typical 5-year-old with no evidence of disease. However, we know the chance of relapse is still high, so we do what we can to continue to raise funds and awareness for childhood cancer.

I met Gretchen at the Mama's Night Out fundraiser in Santa Cruz, California. She is truly an inspiration to me as she continues to pave the way for pediatric cancer research. She could have stopped her crusade once her beautiful Prince Liam passed away, but she didn't. I know she does not like to consider herself an "inspiration" to others but, bottom line—she is. I will be forever grateful to her for starting Cookies for Kids' Cancer

and giving all our kids today a fighting chance to live! Ty was lucky to benefit from a clinical trial only offered at Memorial Sloan-Kettering Cancer Center, one of the cancer centers that Cookies supports by funding research for new clinical trials, which I believe are the saving grace for many children in treatment.

My co-workers at Santa Clara County Probation Department have been extremely supportive ever since Ty was diagnosed. They donated over 2,000 of their vacation hours so I could care for my son 24/7 throughout his grueling treatment.

These same colleagues always encouraged me to hold a Cookies for Kids' Cancer bake sale at work. All of us banded together and did it, raising over $1,500. Lots of people just came by and donated money without buying anything. We also sold at least 75 dozen preorder cookies the week before, boosting our total to $2,541.

My co-workers keep asking if I will be doing another Cookies for Kids' Cancer bake sale, and my response has always been, "Yes!" In honor of my hero, Ty, and all his cancer friends, we will continue to do our part and raise funds and awareness.

Bay Minette, AL

KIM COOPER & LESLIE McCRANEY/COOKIE MOM'STERS
Bay Minette, AL

In real estate, the most important consideration is "location, location, location." The same holds true for a bake sale. When we decided to host a Cookies for Kids' Cancer event, we knew that where we set up shop for the day was key. The pavilion at our local ball park, right on the main road in town fit the bill. Not only would we be visible to local residents attending a scheduled youth baseball tournament but also to tourists heading to the Gulf Shores.

We solicited donations of baked goods from community members and local bakeries with flyers around town and through our Facebook page. We also rounded up donations of silent auction items (at least 25) and sold raffle tickets for a cash prize. Sending out several media releases resulted in two newspaper interviews and an appearance on a local morning television show. We also made it on to the community calendars of three nearby radio stations.

On the Big Day, we had "extras" beyond baked goods to lure a big crowd. Live music courtesy of a local musician. Face painting. A bounce house. A clown making balloon shapes. The Gulf Coast Tumblebus (a mobile gymnastics play area). And finally, what I feel was one of the biggest draws: a guest appearance by University of Alabama quarterback AJ McCarron, who spent about 3 hours signing autographs and posing for pictures. He also signed a football, a jersey, and a silkscreen banner that we auctioned off. (Just those three items brought in $1,000.) When it came time to draw the raffles, a local cancer warrior did the honors. To further raise awareness, we displayed posters with pictures of other local kids in the fight, as well as Liam Witt and several others across the country.

One thing that I feel increased our sales was that we used a "Square," which is a portable credit card reader. We racked up almost $450 in sales in credit cards alone! Bake sale hosts should definitely look into this to up their total.

peanut butter nanaimo bars

yield: 4 dozen bars

Named for Nanaimo, British Columbia, these bars are a Canadian sweet that is hugely popular all over North America. A no-bake delight, our version has a fairly typical crust and top, but we added creamy peanut butter to the filling.

for the crust

1½ cups graham cracker crumbs

1 cup sweetened flaked coconut

½ cup chopped walnuts

2 ounces (two squares) semi-sweet chocolate, chopped

1 stick (¼ pound) unsalted butter

for the filling

1 stick (¼ pound) unsalted butter, at room temperature

¾ cup smooth peanut butter

⅔ cup confectioners' sugar

for the topping

2 ounces (two squares) semi-sweet chocolate, chopped

1 tablespoon unsalted butter

- Line a 9 x 9-inch pan with foil.
- **To make the crust:** Place the graham cracker crumbs, coconut, and walnuts in a medium bowl. Place the chocolate and butter in a glass bowl and microwave on high for 1 minute, stirring after 30 seconds. When chocolate is melted, add to the crumb mixture and mix well. Press crumb mixture into bottom of prepared pan. Refrigerate for at least 30 minutes.
- **To make the filling:** Place the butter and peanut butter in mixer bowl and beat until creamy, about 1 minute. With the mixer on low, add the confectioners' sugar and beat until creamy and well blended. Spread evenly on the crust and refrigerate for at least 30 minutes.
- **To make topping:** Place the chocolate and butter in a glass bowl and microwave on high for 1 minute, stirring after 30 seconds. When the

chocolate is melted, carefully spread over the peanut butter layer. Refrigerate for several hours to set the chocolate.

- Using a hot, straight-edged knife, cut in 16 equal squares, then cut each square into 3 bars.
- Store in the refrigerator for up to 3 days. Do not freeze.

not the "bake sale" type? ❋ other ways to be a good cookie

- Host a holiday cookie exchange that gives back! Invite a couple dozen friends, have everyone bring cookies to exchange, and encourage everyone to drop a donation in the Cookies for Kids' Cancer Donation Jar.
- Ask a business to do a "Cookies Night" with a percentage of sales going to Cookies for Kids' Cancer—it is an easy event to promote with no baking involved, and it raises money and awareness at the same time—a win-win for all.
- School soccer or basketball tournaments or club lacrosse teams can host a fundraiser while playing the sport they love.
- Take a basket of baked goods to your office and set out a donation jar. Your co-workers will be happy to take a treat knowing they're giving to a great cause!
- Cookies make the perfect wedding, baby shower, or birthday party favor. Bake and package them yourself and make a donation online for the honorees, or order directly from Cookies for Kids' Cancer for gourmet cookies baked and shipped to your special event.

checkerboard slices

yield: 2½ dozen cookies

No one will know that to make these strikingly cool-looking cookies, all you had to do was add some flour and cocoa powder to a package of refrigerated sugar cookie dough.

One 16.5-ounce package refrigerated sugar cookie dough	1 tablespoon Hershey's Special Dark Unsweetened Cocoa Powder
7 tablespoons all-purpose flour, divided	2 tablespoons mini chocolate chips (optional)

- Divide the cookie dough in half. Knead 4 tablespoons of the flour into half of the dough. Knead 3 tablespoons of the flour and the cocoa powder into the other half of the dough. Knead mini chocolate chips into white dough, if using.

- Divide each piece of the dough into 4 equal pieces. Roll each piece into a 4-inch log. Place one white and one chocolate log next to each other, then place a white log on the chocolate log, and a chocolate log on the white, forming the checkerboard pattern. Wrap in plastic wrap and refrigerate for at least 1 hour and up to 3 days. Repeat with the remaining 4 logs.

- Preheat the oven to 350°F. Line 2 cookie sheets with parchment paper.

- Slice each log of chilled dough in ¼-inch thick slices and place about 2 inches apart on the prepared cookie sheets.

- Transfer to the oven and bake until the cookies begin to brown at the edges, 10 to 12 minutes, rotating the cookie sheets on the oven racks halfway through the baking time. Cool on the cookie sheets for 3 minutes. Transfer to wire racks to cool completely. Repeat with the remaining dough on cool cookie sheets.

- Store in an airtight container for up to 3 days, or freeze for up to 3 months.

lovie's seven-layer bars

yield: 4 dozen bars

Our last book had a five-layer bar, so we figured we needed to up the ante. Lovie, a dear friend of Fraya's, always made these, so Fraya never had to. Once she did, she realized how ridiculously easy it is to get seven yums in treats to sell at a bake sale. That's why they're here in our make-it-fast chapter.

½ stick (2 ounces) unsalted butter, melted

1 cup graham cracker crumbs

One 7-ounce bag sweetened flaked coconut

1 cup (6 ounces) chocolate chips

1 cup (6 ounces) butterscotch chips

One 14-ounce can sweetened condensed milk

1 cup chopped nuts such as pecans, walnuts, or toasted almonds

- Preheat the oven to 325°F. Line a 9 x 13-inch baking pan with foil.
- Spread the melted butter in the bottom of the lined baking pan. Sprinkle the graham cracker crumbs over the butter. Top the crumbs with coconut. Sprinkle the chocolate and butterscotch chips on top of the coconut. Pour the condensed milk over the entire pan and top with nuts.
- Transfer to the oven and bake 40 to 50 minutes. Cool completely in the pan on a wire rack. Remove from the pan and cut in 48 pieces.
- Store in an airtight container for up to 3 days, or freeze for up to 3 months.

packaging ideas ✻ Chinese takeout boxes make great packaging. They could be your perfect solution for large cupcakes or oversized muffins.

sensational cookies

almond oatmeal cookies

yield: about 3 dozen cookies

Beth Lipton, food director at *All You* magazine, is totally inspired by what her longtime friend Gretchen accomplished with Cookies for Kids' Cancer. And we are totally inspired by Beth's tender oatmeal cookie that brings chocolaty, nutty, coconut candy bar yum to every bite.

½ cup sweetened flaked coconut

¾ cup whole-wheat pastry or all-purpose flour

½ teaspoon baking soda

¼ teaspoon salt

1 stick (¼ pound) unsalted butter, at room temperature

⅔ cup light or dark brown sugar

1 large egg, at room temperature

1 teaspoon vanilla extract

1½ cups old-fashioned or quick-cooking oats

1 cup (6 ounces) dark chocolate chips

½ cup chopped almonds, toasted (see Tip page 32)

- Preheat the oven to 250°F.
- Spread the coconut evenly on a cookie sheet, transfer to the oven, and bake until just golden, about 10 minutes. Let cool on the cookie sheet.
- Place the flour, baking soda, and salt in a bowl and mix well. Set aside.
- Place the butter and brown sugar in a large mixer bowl and beat until smooth and creamy, about 3 minutes. Add the egg and vanilla and beat well. Scrape down the sides of the bowl. With the mixer on low, add the flour mixture and beat just until combined. Stir in oats, chocolate chips, almonds, oats, and coconut. Refrigerate for at least 1 hour and up to 2 days.
- Preheat the oven to 350°F. Line 2 cookie sheets with parchment paper.
- Using a level small (2-teaspoon size) cookie scoop, drop the dough about 2 inches apart on the prepared cookie sheets.

- Transfer to the oven and bake until the cookies begin to brown at the edges, 12 to 14 minutes, rotating the cookie sheets on the oven racks halfway through the baking time. Cool on the cookie sheets for 5 minutes. Transfer to wire racks and cool completely. Repeat with the remaining dough on cool cookie sheets.

- Store in an airtight container for up to 3 days, or freeze for up to 3 months.

packaging ideas ✿ Use your choice of grosgrain color ribbon to take your packaging to the next level. Step 1: Enclose cookies in a resealable bag (included in bake sale kit). Step 2: Cut enough ribbon to wrap around the package. Step 3: Place Cookies logo sticker on top of where the two ends of ribbon meet. This is a great way to incorporate colors that match your event (school colors, sports team colors, etc.).

just for fun ✿ Ask local mascots to make an appearance—sports teams and local restaurants often have mascots that can make an appearance and add to the fun, or leave a large blow-up mascot to draw attention.

get organized ✿ Make your bake sale travel with wagons! Send a wagonload of goodies and a donation jar out into a crowd to reach more people and keep your volunteers moving.

coconut pecan balls

yield: about 6 dozen cookies

For coconut lovers everywhere, these have it all. Coconut coats the cookie that hides the surprise inside: a pecan half. Once baked, the flavors meld together perfectly. Yum!

for the cookies

2 sticks (½ pound) unsalted butter, at room temperature

¾ cup granulated sugar

1 tablespoon vanilla extract

2 cups all-purpose flour

½ teaspoon salt

1½ cups (6 ounces) pecan halves

for coconut coating

1 large egg white, at room temperature

1 tablespoon water

1¼ cups sweetened flaked coconut

- Preheat the oven to 350°F. Line 2 cookie sheets with parchment paper.
- **To make the cookies:** Place the butter and sugar in a large mixer bowl and beat until smooth and creamy, about 3 minutes. Add the vanilla and beat well. With the mixer on low, gradually add the flour and salt and beat until well combined.
- Shape a level small (2-teaspoon size) cookie scoop of the dough around each pecan half to form balls.
- **To make the coconut coating:** Place the egg white and water in a shallow bowl and beat to combine. Place the coconut on a plate.
- With a fork, dip the dough balls in the egg white mixture, then in coconut, coating well. Place on the prepared cookie sheets, 2 inches apart. Bake until the cookies begin to brown, 14 to 16 minutes, rotating the cookie sheets on the oven racks halfway through the baking time. Cool on the cookie sheets for 3 minutes. Transfer to wire racks and cool completely. Repeat with the remaining dough on cool cookie sheets.
- Store in an airtight container for up to 3 days, or freeze for up to 3 months.

lemon wheels

yield: about 6 dozen cookies

With zip from fresh lemon and tenderness from butter and cream cheese, these lemon slices are wheely, wheely good.

2 sticks (½ pound) unsalted butter, at room temperature

3 ounces cream cheese, at room temperature

1 cup granulated sugar

1 large egg, at room temperature

1 tablespoon fresh lemon juice

2 teaspoons freshly grated lemon zest

3 cups all-purpose flour

Yellow and white nonpareil candy sprinkles

- Place the butter and cream cheese in a large mixer bowl and beat until smooth and creamy, about 3 minutes. Add the sugar and beat until fluffy. Add the egg, lemon juice, and lemon zest one at a time, beating after each addition. Scrape down the sides of the bowl. With the mixer on low, slowly add the flour and beat until well combined.

- Divide the dough into quarters. Shape each quarter into a 1¾-inch-diameter log and roll in sprinkles to coat. Cover each log and refrigerate for at least 4 hours and up to 3 days.

- Preheat the oven to 350°F. Line 2 cookie sheets with parchment paper.

- With the tip of a very sharp knife, cut each log into ¼-inch slices. Place on the prepared cookie sheets, 2 inches apart. Transfer to the oven and bake until the cookies just begin to brown on the edges, 10 to 12 minutes, rotating the cookie sheets on the oven racks halfway through the baking time. Cool on the cookie sheets for 3 minutes. Transfer to wire racks and cool completely. Repeat with the remaining dough on cool cookie sheets.

- Store in an airtight container for up to 3 days, or freeze for up to 3 months.

Tinton Falls, NJ

KIMBERLY ROSEN AND FAMILY
Tinton Falls, NJ

- -

On a Saturday morning, our team of dedicated Good Cookies came together to host our 4th Annual Cookies for Kids' Cancer Bake Sale at the Jersey Shore Premium Outlets in Tinton Falls, New Jersey. Year after year they allow us to come and host our event in this bustling shopping center at the heart of the holiday shopping season. And this year proved to be just as successful, as we raised nearly $2,500 for the 4th year in a row.

Our event featured nearly 1,000 homemade cookies that were baked and packaged by many volunteers who also came out and donated to the bake sale. Our host team—consisting mostly of children ranging from age 3 to 11—did an amazing job in getting the attention of the public with cute signs, balloons, and table decorations.

For 4 years we have joyfully supported Cookies for Kids' Cancer. For the love of our children and the love of all children, we're inspired to make a difference.

REBECCA GILES
Malibu, CA

- -

Before I entered medical school, I spent 2 years volunteering in the bone marrow transplant unit of Stanford's Packard Children's Hospital. The experience I had with those sick kids and their families changed me indelibly. Now that I'm a mom, I feel their heartbreak more deeply, and my memories of that time are more poignant. This cause is very dear to my heart, and as an avid baker, combining fundraising with cookies makes perfect sense to me.

I held a Cookies for Kids' Cancer Bake Sale on an unusually gloomy December day at the Malibu Country Mart in Malibu, California. My friends and I battled the cold with thermoses full of hot chocolate and lots of holiday cheer. Despite the weather, more than 300 locals came out to support Cookies for Kids' Cancer—fellow moms, celebrities, and even retired corporate titans! My friend LeAnn Rimes and her husband Eddie Cibrian brought their boys to gobble up cookies and support the cause. LeAnn helped publicize the sale by tweeting about it days before the event. At the day's end our bodies were frozen but our hearts were warm: We had raised a little over $5,000 for Cookies for Kids' Cancer. Lesson learned: make more shortbread! It sold out too fast.

New York, NY

JESSI BRELSFORD/TASTE BUDS
New York, NY

Taste Buds offers cooking classes and events for kids. Last summer during our week-long camps, Thursday was our bake day and we made sure to turn it into more than just a lesson on proper measurements. Every Thursday during the summer between 11:30 and 3:30 in front of our building located in the heart of Manhattan, we hosted a Cookies for Kids' Cancer bake sale.

We wanted the kids to really feel like they were a pivotal part of helping other kids who were sick, so we walked them through everything from A to Z. We taught the kids about bake sales, Cookies for Kids' Cancer, and what it means to raise money for pediatric cancer research. After going over all of the details, we took to the kitchen to whip up our bake sale items of the day—usually brownies and cookies. The kids loved making the sweet treats for a good cause. While the treats were in the oven, the kids teamed together to make a huge bake sale sign and then we all packaged the cookies together. We then packed up our "bake sale box" and headed down to the street to set up our table.

The kids loved it! They all loved being in charge of the money box and were so excited to be helping others! The next morning at camp, we'd count how much we raised and donate it right away to our friends at Cookies for Kids' Cancer. Our bake sales were definitely the highlight of the week for many campers!

To date, we've raised nearly $4,000 for Cookies for Kids' Cancer, plus we made a bake sale video that we shared on our website as a way to teach others how easy and fun it is to host a bake sale for Cookies for Kids' Cancer!

boston cream whoopie pies

yield: 2 dozen large or 4 dozen small

oston cream pie isn't really pie, and whoopie pies aren't either, so it made perfect ironic sense to get them together. Keep the fluffy vanilla pudding cold and fill them to order, or keep them refrigerated.

for the cookies

2 sticks (½ pound) unsalted butter, at room temperature

½ teaspoon salt

1 tablespoon vanilla extract

1 tablespoon baking powder

1¼ cups granulated sugar

3 large eggs, at room temperature

4½ cups all-purpose flour

1 cup milk

for the filling

1 cup cold milk

1 package (3 ounces) instant vanilla pudding

1 stick (¼ pound) unsalted butter, at room temperature

1 cup marshmallow creme (Fluff)

for the glaze

2 cups (12 ounces) chocolate chips

1 cup heavy or whipping cream

- Preheat the oven to 400°F. Line 2 cookie sheets with parchment paper.

- **To make the cookies:** Place the butter, salt, vanilla, baking powder, and sugar in a large mixer bowl and beat until smooth and creamy, about 3 minutes. Add the eggs one at a time, beating after each addition. Add one-third of the flour (1½ cups) and beat, then add half of the milk and beat. Continue alternating flour with milk, finishing with flour. Scrape down the sides of the bowl.

- Using either a medium or large cookie scoop, drop the dough about 2 inches apart on the prepared cookie sheets.

- Transfer to the oven and bake until the cookies are just set, 10 to 12 minutes, rotating the cookie sheets on the oven racks halfway through the baking time. Cool on the cookie sheets for 3 minutes. Transfer to wire racks to cool completely. Repeat with the remaining dough on cool cookie sheets.

- **To make the filling:** Place the cold milk in medium bowl, whisk in the instant pudding, and continue to whip for 2 minutes. Refrigerate for 30 minutes. In mixer bowl, beat the butter until creamy, about 2 minutes. Beat in the chilled pudding, scrape down the sides of the bowl, and beat in marshmallow creme. Refrigerate for 2 hours, or up to 2 days.

- **To make the glaze:** Place chocolate chips in a medium glass bowl. In a small saucepan, bring the cream to a boil. Pour over the chocolate and stir until melted. Microwave for 10 seconds at a time if chocolate isn't completely melted. Cool slightly.

- **To assemble whoopie pies:** Place a cooling rack in a baking pan. Place half of the cooled cookies on the rack and coat with the glaze. Scoop chilled filling onto unglazed cookies, 1 tablespoon onto small cookies, 2 tablespoons onto large. Top with glazed cookies. Refrigerate until ready to serve.

- Store filled cookies in the refrigerator for up to 1 day. Do not freeze.

granola bars

yield: 40 bars

Just the thing for an early morning bake sale: a bar that can fill in for breakfast. Every mom on the block will be happy to see a homemade granola bar made with nuts, oats, and fruit.

½ cup almond butter, at room temperature

1 stick (¼ pound) unsalted butter, melted

¼ cup honey

2 tablespoons corn syrup

1 tablespoon water

2 teaspoons vanilla extract

1¾ cups quick-cooking oats

½ cup all-purpose flour

¼ cup granulated sugar

2½ cups chopped dried fruit and nuts

½ cup cinnamon chips

- Preheat the oven to 350°F. Line a 9 x 13-inch baking pan with foil.
- Place the almond butter, butter, honey, corn syrup, water, and vanilla in a large mixer bowl and beat until well combined. Place the oats, flour, sugar, chopped fruit and nuts, and the cinnamon chips in a separate bowl; mix well and add to butter mixture. Stir until everything is well incorporated.
- Spread evenly in the prepared pan, pressing firmly. Transfer to the oven and bake just until edges are browned, 30 minutes. Cool in the pan on a wire rack for 10 minutes. Remove from pan, cut into 40 bars and cool completely.
- Store in an airtight container for up to 3 days, or freeze for up to 3 months.

spread the word ❀ Reach out to a local public relations firm to help write a press release and get the attention of local media and businesses.

sour cream drops

yield: about 5 dozen cookies

Just the right amount of sour (from the sour cream) balances out the sweet in these simple, soft cookies.

1½ sticks (6 ounces) unsalted butter, at room temperature

1½ cups granulated sugar

2 large eggs, at room temperature

1 tablespoon vanilla extract

1 teaspoon freshly grated lemon zest

3 cups all-purpose flour

½ teaspoon baking powder

½ teaspoon baking soda

½ teaspoon salt

1 cup sour cream

Rainbow sprinkles

- Preheat the oven to 350°F. Line 2 cookie sheets with parchment paper.

- Place the butter and sugar in a large mixer bowl and beat until smooth and creamy, about 3 minutes. Add the eggs, vanilla, and lemon zest, one at a time, beating well after each addition. Scrape down the sides of the bowl. Place the flour, baking powder, baking soda, and salt in a separate bowl and mix well. With the mixer on low, add the flour mixture to the butter mixture, alternating with sour cream, and beat until combined. Scrape down the sides of the bowl again and beat to combine.

- Using a level small (2-teaspoon size) cookie scoop, drop the dough about 2 inches apart on the prepared cookie sheets. Top with sprinkles.

- Transfer to the oven and bake until the edges of the cookies are lightly browned, 11 to 13 minutes, rotating the cookie sheets on the oven racks halfway through the baking time. Cool on the cookie sheets for 3 minutes. Transfer to wire racks and cool completely. Repeat with the remaining dough on cool cookie sheets.

- Store in an airtight container for up to 3 days, or freeze for up to 3 months.

swedish walnut crisps

yield: 2 dozen cookie wedges

Buttery, thin, crisp, and encrusted with nuts: our idea of heaven. We love the wedges, but a standard jelly-roll pan will work if you don't have a pizza pan.

2 sticks (½ pound) unsalted butter, at room temperature

1 cup granulated sugar

2 large eggs, separated, at room temperature

2 teaspoons vanilla extract

½ teaspoon salt

2½ cups all-purpose flour

½ cup light brown sugar

1¼ cups chopped walnuts

1 teaspoon freshly grated lemon zest

- Preheat the oven to 350°F.
- Place the butter and granulated sugar in a large mixer bowl and beat until smooth and creamy, about 3 minutes. Add the 2 egg yolks, vanilla, and salt one at a time, beating after each addition. Scrape down the sides of the bowl. With the mixer on low, add the flour and beat well; scrape down the sides of the bowl again. Press the dough evenly into an ungreased pizza pan (14-inch round).
- Place the 2 egg whites in the bowl of a mixer fitted with a whisk and beat until soft peaks form, 3 to 4 minutes. Add brown sugar, walnuts, and lemon zest, gently stirring to combine. Spread walnut mixture on top of the dough. Transfer to the oven and bake until the edges of the dough are lightly browned and egg whites are dry, 30 minutes. Immediately cut into 24 wedges using a pizza wheel and cool completely in the pan on a wire rack.
- Store in an airtight container for up to 3 days, or freeze for up to 3 months.

Louisville, CO

KATE MEYERS
Louisville, CO

Sometimes you just have to put it out there and trust the universe . . .

That was my thinking when I organized my first cookie exchange. I chose Valentine's Day to honor the birthday of Sam Johnson, my close friend Kate's wonderful son who died of a brain tumor at age 5. When I heard about the amazing Gretchen Holt and Cookies for Kids' Cancer, I felt compelled to try to help. The organization Gretchen started has already raised millions of dollars.

So here's what I say: "Every cookie counts!!"

I reached out to family and friends with the idea for everyone to bake 10 dozen cookies. We would meet at my house for a party the Sunday before Valentine's Day, assemble bags of mixed cookies, then sell them for $10 a dozen.

About 10 days before the cookie exchange, one person in my circle sent regrets for the party and a check for $100. I actually started crying—from then on, I knew that we were starting something wonderful.

That Sunday, my crew outdid itself. Jenny bested Martha Stewart with her linzer tortes. The kids started an assembly line, with Thayer, our youngest volunteer at age 8, filling the largest number of bags and Kristen and Katie helping tie ribbons on all of them. Sue baked at the last minute. Dana drove from Boulder even though her daughter was sick and she knew no one at the party. M. C. brought good cheer, extra tables, and her beautiful daughters. And Jaimi helped with math, photography, and cookies. I could go on, but I think you get the embarrassment of riches that surrounded me, and I am both humbled and proud to report that we raised $1,995.

I'd like to expand to more cities next year. My sister-in-law Michelle volunteered for Pittsburgh, and my friend Julie will corral a Birmingham contingent. If you're up for doing a Valentine Cookie sale where you live, we'd be thrilled to have you join our ranks. Love, cookies, friendship, a little red candy, and fundraising for an important cause—talk about a pretty perfect equation.

OXO
New York, NY

"OXOnians," as OXO employees affectionately refer to one another, regard each other as family. Together we celebrate birthdays, weddings, and anniversaries just like we would with friends and loved ones. On May 13, 2004, we were overcome with excitement at the arrival of Liam Witt, the beautiful son of two longtime OXOnians, Gretchen and Larry Witt. On January 24, 2011, we were overcome with grief at his passing.

Liam was a fixture in our office. He instinctively followed OXO's philosophy to question everything and was always willing (sometimes too willing) to test products. Liam could always be counted on for constructive, honest feedback. He often raced OXO's president, Alex Lee, on scooters around the office, legitimately beating him most of the time!

His smile and laugh live on in the memory of everyone at OXO.

When Gretchen had the idea for a larger-than-life bake sale in December 2007, OXOnians rallied together to support her efforts. We were there alongside Gretchen and Larry as they sold 96,000 cookies and raised over $420,000. When that larger-than-life bake sale turned into Cookies for Kids' Cancer, OXOnians did whatever we could to help—bake cookies, write thank-you letters, tie ribbons, and of course, host an annual bake sale.

Each year, preparations for our bake sale begin months in advance. We secure several prime spots in our 18-story office building. We visit every office to invite others to attend. We advertise our sale to our 100,000 Facebook fans and Twitter followers. We ask for donations from the best bakeries in New York City. And we bake.

In the days leading up to our bake sale, the entire office smells of mouthwatering cookies, cupcakes, bread, pastries, you name it. OXOnians form assembly lines for baking, stuffing bags, stickering, packing boxes, and transporting to the sale. Snacking is allowed . . . for a price—a donation to Cookies for Kids' Cancer.

As we sell and ask for donations, we are humbled by the statistics but proud to spread the word. Our favorite moment is when people are so moved by Liam's story that they ask the golden question, "How can I get involved?" Through the years, OXOnians have helped raise close to $500,000 for Cookies for Kids' Cancer, but our proudest moment is knowing we have inspired others to do their part.

chai stars

yield: 4 to 12 dozen, depending on size of cookie cutter

G rinding tea from a couple of chai tea bags puts the warm coziness of a chai latte in a crisp, buttery cut-out cookie.

for the cookies

2 tablespoons granulated sugar

2 chai tea bags

2 sticks (½ pound) unsalted butter, at room temperature

1 cup light brown sugar

½ teaspoon vanilla extract

½ teaspoon baking soda

Pinch salt

2½ cups all-purpose flour

for the glaze

1½ tablespoons water or brewed chai tea

1½ cups confectioners' sugar

- **To make the cookies:** Place the granulated sugar and loose tea from 2 chai tea bags in a spice grinder and grind until fine. Place in mixer bowl with the butter, brown sugar, vanilla, baking soda, and salt and beat until smooth and creamy, about 4 minutes. With the mixer on low, add the flour and mix to blend thoroughly.

- Divide the dough in half, flatten into disks, and wrap in plastic wrap. Refrigerate for at least 1 hour and up to 2 days.

- Preheat the oven to 375°F. Line 2 cookie sheets with parchment paper.

- On a lightly floured surface roll the dough ⅛ inch thick. Using a star cookie cutter, cut out shapes and place 1 inch apart on the prepared cookie sheets. Re-roll scraps, chilling dough if necessary.

- Transfer to the oven and bake until the cookies begin to brown at the edges, 8 to 10 minutes, rotating the cookie sheets on the oven racks halfway through the baking time. Cool on the cookie sheets for 3 minutes. Transfer to wire racks to cool completely. Repeat with the remaining dough on cool cookie sheets.

- **To make the glaze**: Mix water or brewed chai tea with the confectioners' sugar to make a glaze. Place the glaze in resealable plastic bag, snip off a corner, and decorate cooled cookies.
- Store in an airtight container for up to 3 days, or freeze for up to 3 months.

tips from top hosts
✿ JEN BAKI, ANCHORAGE, AK

Your community wants to support you and your cause.

People are basically kindhearted, but store owners are also business-oriented. To get donations you have to do two things: tug on their heartstrings and present to them why donating to this cause would benefit them. Often we needed to visit a business two or three times before we got a donation, but we chose not to take "no" or "I'll think about it" for an answer.

spread the word ✿ During the week of your event, ask your friends to advertise for you by writing the details on their car windows with window chalk.

piña colada cookies

yield: 5 dozen cookies

No alcohol involved, so even the kids can dig in. Sweet pineapple and coconut scream "cocktail!" in these tender cookies.

2 sticks (½ pound) unsalted butter, at room temperature

1 cup granulated sugar

½ teaspoon baking soda

2 large eggs, at room temperature

1 teaspoon vanilla extract

2⅔ cups all-purpose flour

1 cup diced dried pineapple

2 cups sweetened flaked coconut, divided

½ cup chopped macadamia nuts

- Place the butter, sugar, and baking soda in a large mixer bowl and beat until smooth and creamy, about 3 minutes. Add the eggs one at a time, beating after each addition, and the vanilla.

- With the mixer on low, gradually add the flour; beat until well incorpo rated. Scrape down the sides of the bowl; add the pineapple, 1 cup of the coconut, and macadamia nuts and mix again. Refrigerate the dough for 1 hour or up to 3 days.

- Preheat the oven to 325°F. Line 2 cookie sheets with parchment paper.

- Place the remaining 1 cup of coconut in a food processor and pulse to fine crumbs.

- Using a level small (2-teaspoon size) cookie scoop, drop the dough into the coconut crumbs. Roll to coat. Place the cookies about 2 inches apart on the prepared cookie sheets.

- Transfer to the oven and bake until the cookies begin to brown at the edges, 9 to 11 minutes, rotating the cookie sheets on the oven racks half-way through the baking time. Cool on the cookie sheets for 3 minutes. Transfer to wire racks to cool completely. Repeat with the remaining dough on cool cookie sheets.

- Store in an airtight container for up to 3 days, or freeze for up to 3 months.

moya's oatmeal raisinet cookies

yield: about 6 dozen cookies

When Jackie's daughter Moya was little, oatmeal cookies and Raisinets were her two faves, so we mixed them together! Fraya's son Eli thought they were so good he suggested we "put this recipe in the book twice."

2 sticks (½ pound) unsalted butter, at room temperature	1½ cups all-purpose flour
¾ cup light brown sugar	1 teaspoon baking soda
½ cup granulated sugar	½ teaspoon salt
2 large eggs, at room temperature	½ teaspoon ground cinnamon
1½ teaspoons vanilla extract	3 cups quick-cooking oats
	1½ cups Raisinets
	1 cup chopped walnuts

- Preheat the oven to 350°F. Line 2 cookie sheets with parchment paper.

- Place the butter and sugars in a large mixer bowl and beat until smooth and creamy, about 3 minutes. Add the eggs and vanilla, one at a time, beating after each addition.

- Place the flour, baking soda, salt, and cinnamon in a separate bowl; mix well and add to the butter mixture. Beat until everything is well incorporated. Scrape down the sides of the bowl, add the oats, and mix again. Add the Raisinets and nuts and stir to combine.

- Drop the dough using a heaping small (2-teaspoon size) cookie scoop, about 2 inches apart on the prepared cookie sheets.

- Transfer to the oven and bake until the cookies begin to brown at the edges, 10 to 12 minutes, rotating the cookie sheets on the oven racks halfway through the baking time. Cool on the cookie sheets for 3 minutes. Transfer to wire racks to cool completely. Repeat with the remaining dough on cool cookie sheets.

- Store in an airtight container for up to 3 days, or freeze for up to 3 months.

HOUGH HIGH SCHOOL SOCCER PROGRAM
Cornelius, NC

- -

I've known Grier Christenbury's parents since high school. Watching Grier and his family as he's battled pediatric cancer for over 5 years reminds me just how carefree high school really is. And now, as a high school soccer coach, I know how lucky these kids are to be healthy and I also know that some of them might be friends for life. So it seemed like the right thing to do to support the cause the Christenburys care so much about by hosting the Cookies for Kids' Cancer/Hough Soccer Invitational Soccer Tournament.

The tournament was an all-day event held on a Saturday at Hough High School Stadium. Between 500 and 600 people attended, which was key since a portion of the ticket sales went directly toward the cause. The tournament featured 4 games of men's high school soccer with top teams from Charlotte, Winston-Salem, and Asheville.

In addition to the fun of the sport on a perfect September afternoon, the bake sale kept the crowd from getting hungry. With lots of cookies and brownies and cupcakes to pick from, everyone had the chance to find something they liked. In the end, we raised over $3,200 for

Cookies for Kids' Cancer—and we're planning on making this an annual event.

Mahopac, NY

TONTA (ROBBI) GALBRAITH
Mahopac, NY

- -

We created the first of its kind Cookies for Kids' Cancer Bachelor/ Bachelorette Auction/Bake Sale! We wanted to do something fun and different and it was a blast! We had 4 guys and 4 girls, which was perfect. They got into the spirit of the event and made it huge!

Our emcee really got things going. We auctioned the bachelors/ bachelorettes and then had a silent auction where we auctioned off a guitar, which people went crazy over. We also auctioned off Yankees memorabilia and a summer camp registration for a child, plus restaurant gift certificates, gym memberships, gift baskets, hair salon certificates, and a 50/50 raffle. A local band was just phenomenal at entertaining us for the evening!

I've never done an auction before and it was so amazing to see how excited people were and how willing they were to bid for these items. Next time I'm going even bigger!

Anchorage, AK

JEN BAKI
Anchorage, AK

Bryant Ante, a local boy, was enjoying life like any happy 6-year-old when the lump in his neck turned out to be cancer. He immediately began aggressive treatment at Seattle Children's Hospital, and despite countless needle pokes, long hospital stays and a daunting medication regimen, Bryant remained strong, brave, and NEVER complained about his life. Every morning that Bryant woke up—sick and exhausted—he greeted each day with a smile and lived it as though it could be his last, just as a true hero would. To everyone's joy, Bryant was declared cancer-free on June 1, 2009. But sadly, within weeks, cancer came back, this time in his spinal fluid. Everyone rallied around Bryant and prayed that he could beat this disease a second time, but it was not to be. We lost Bryant on July 10, 2009. In his memory, a bunch of us who had followed his journey decided to raise money for Cookies for Kids' Cancer.

A group known as Bryant's Good Cookies hosted the first-ever Great Alaska Cookie Bake Off. Generous, kind-hearted members of our Anchorage community came out in droves to listen to live music, bid during a silent auction, and cast votes for Anchorage's Best Cookie, a head-to-head competition among a number of the city's top restaurants and bakeries. As pro chefs vied for the coveted title, we shared eye-opening facts about pediatric cancer. The cookies gave guests a lot of food for thought and plenty to talk about, since everyone had an opinion. The night was a huge success, not only because we raised a good amount of money, $9,500, but because the community came together and put forth a true philanthropic effort.

The next cookie challenge promises to be even more exciting, and we hope that with the community coming together, we can exceed our goal of raising more than $25,000.

poppy seed cookies

yield: about 5 dozen cookies

Making these not-very-sweet cookies is a Berg family tradition, so much so that anyone who has ever had one assumed Fraya would put them in this book. Crisp, flavorful—and addicting.

2 large eggs, at room temperature

½ cup granulated sugar

⅓ cup vegetable oil

1 teaspoon vanilla extract

¼ teaspoon almond extract

⅔ cup poppy seeds

2¾ cups all-purpose flour

1 teaspoon baking powder

¼ teaspoon baking soda

- Preheat the oven to 375°F. Line 2 cookie sheets with parchment paper.
- Place the eggs and sugar in a large mixer bowl and beat until light and smooth, about 3 minutes. Add the oil, vanilla and almond extracts, and poppy seeds and beat well.
- Place the flour, baking powder, and baking soda in a separate bowl; mix well and add to the egg mixture. Beat until everything is well incorporated. Scrape down the sides of the bowl and mix again.
- Divide the dough into 3 balls. Roll each ball of the dough ⅛ inch thick and cut with a 2¼- to 2½-inch round fluted cookie cutter. Place on the prepared cookie sheets, ½ inch apart. Bake until golden brown, 10 to 15 minutes, rotating the cookie sheets on the oven racks halfway through the baking time. Cool on the cookie sheets for 3 minutes. Transfer to wire racks to cool completely. Repeat with the remaining dough on cool cookie sheets.
- Store in an airtight container for up to 5 days, or freeze for up to 3 months.

toffee-almond meringues

yield: 2 dozen cookies

One bite of these sweet and nutty air puffs of a cookie and our six-year-old friend's reaction was "These are so good I can't stand it!" His mom is French, and she says they are as good as any she's ever had. We consider that high praise indeed.

3 large egg whites, at room temperature

¼ teaspoon fresh lemon juice

¾ cup granulated sugar

½ teaspoon vanilla extract

¾ cup Heath toffee bits

1 cup chopped almonds, toasted (see Tip page 32)

- Preheat the oven to 250°F. Line 2 cookie sheets with parchment paper.
- In a large bowl, whip the egg whites and lemon juice to soft peaks. With the mixer on medium, add the sugar 1 tablespoon at a time, then add the vanilla. Increase the mixer speed to high and beat to stiff, glossy peaks. Using a spatula, gently fold the toffee bits and nuts into the egg whites.
- Using a level medium (1½-tablespoon size) cookie scoop, drop scoops of meringue on the prepared cookie sheets, 2 inches apart. Transfer to the oven and bake for 30 minutes, rotating the cookie sheets on the oven racks halfway through the baking time. Turn the oven off and let the meringues sit in the oven for at least 1 hour to cool and set.
- Store in an airtight container for up to 3 days, or freeze for up to 3 months.

what to offer ❋ Customize the sizes of your goodies to suit everyone's needs. Someone may simply want a cookie or two, while others want an entire coffee cake. Be prepared with extra sealable bags and plastic wrap.

grandma jennie's ruggalah

yield: 4 dozen cookies

Marge Perry is an "auntie", baker, teacher, writer and all around great friend. Her Grandma Jennie's ruggalah are beyond compare. A tangy dough made the traditional way (with yeast and sour cream) is filled with jam, cinnamon and nuts. They are perfection.

1½ cups all-purpose flour

1 teaspoon (½ package) dry yeast

1 stick (¼ pound) unsalted butter, chilled

2 large egg yolks

½ cup sour cream

½ cup finely chopped walnuts

½ cup granulated sugar

1 teaspoon ground cinnamon

¼ cup apricot preserves, melted

- Place the flour and yeast in a medium bowl and whisk to mix well. Cut in butter until well combined.

- Place the egg yolks and sour cream in a bowl and mix well. Using a wooden spoon or spatula, stir sour cream mixture into flour mixture until well blended. Handling gently, form the dough into 6 balls, wrap each in plastic wrap, and refrigerate for at least 8 hours and up to 2 days.

- Preheat the oven to 350°F. Line 2 cookie sheets with parchment paper.

- Combine nuts, sugar, and cinnamon in a bowl. Sprinkle a scant tablespoon of the nut mixture on your work surface and on top of it roll one ball into a 6-inch circle. Brush the circle very lightly with the preserves and sprinkle with 2 tablespoons of the nut mixture. Cut into 8 wedges.

- Roll each wedge from the widest end to the narrowest and place on the prepared cookie sheets. Repeat with remaining ingredients.

- Bake for 20 to 25 minutes, until golden, rotating the cookie sheets on the oven racks halfway through the baking time. Cool on the cookie sheets for 3 minutes. Transfer to wire racks to cool completely.

- Store in an airtight container for up to 2 days, or freeze for up to 3 months.

tropical drops

yield: 4 dozen cookies

I s it possible for a cookie to exude sunshine? We think so. Lemon, pineapple, mango, and papaya all say beaches and fun.

1½ sticks (6 ounces) unsalted butter, at room temperature

½ cup granulated sugar

1 large egg, at room temperature

1 teaspoon freshly grated lemon zest

1 teaspoon vanilla extract

¼ teaspoon salt

2 cups all-purpose flour

1 cup diced dried tropical fruit, such as mango, pineapple, and papaya

1 cup finely crushed potato chips

- Preheat the oven to 350°F. Line 2 cookie sheets with parchment paper.

- Place the butter and sugar in a large mixer bowl and beat until smooth and creamy, about 3 minutes. Add the egg, lemon zest, vanilla, and salt, one at a time, beating after each addition.

- With the mixer on low, add flour and mix well. Scrape down the sides of the bowl, add the dried fruit, and mix again. If dough is very stiff, use a wooden spoon to mix. Place the potato chips in a shallow bowl.

- Drop the dough using a heaping small (2-teaspoon size) cookie scoop into potato chips and roll to coat evenly. Place 2 inches apart on the prepared cookie sheets. Use the palm of your hand to flatten them gently. .

- Transfer to the oven and bake until the cookies begin to brown at the edges, 14 to 16 minutes, rotating the cookie sheets on the oven racks halfway through the baking time. Cool on the cookie sheets for 3 minutes. Transfer to wire racks to cool completely. Repeat with the remaining dough on cool cookie sheets.

- Store in an airtight container for up to 3 days, or freeze for up to 3 months.

TERESA TANNER
Auburn, NY

In November, a team from the Ukrainian National Club (UNC) hosted our first Cookies for Kids' Cancer event. The club is located in Auburn, New York, a community that rallied behind the cause. In one day with 20 volunteers we raised $4,000.

One key to our success was that we met weekly and everyone had a job to do. We pulled the entire event off in a month's time—amazing considering our success. To have that much to do in a short period of time is a total commitment. The UNC has been a part of my life for 25-plus years and the team from the UNC made sure our team had whatever we needed for success. Between our families, friends, and members of the club getting the word out and baking, the bake sale came together so easily.

My son did face painting, and my daughter was one of the volunteers and bakers. My husband cooked the hot dogs. Having my family there and helping made it a special day for me. And when my kids said how proud they were of me, well, that too made it a very special day. It is amazing how doing for others is an awesome feeling. Seems even more so because kids are the center of it all.

The UNC and our team cannot wait to host our 2nd Annual Cookies for Kids' Cancer bake sale next year.

Long Island, NY

RACHEL ROBERGE
Long Island, NY

As a former volunteer on the pediatric floor at Memorial Sloan-Kettering Cancer Center in New York City, I knew I wanted to get involved in the fight against kids' cancer in a big way but wasn't sure how. As a working mom of two, it was difficult to feel like I could make a difference. That changed the moment I found out about Cookies for Kids' Cancer—I knew I wanted to contribute because I identified with their mission to fund cutting-edge research into new and improved treatments for childhood cancer.

When I decided to host my first bake sale, I was excited to teach my daughter and son about the honor and joy in giving back to others. Seeing photographs of children holding up "Kids Helping Kids" signs on the Cookies website made me really want to get going.

So I started the magical journey of planning. I say "magical" because as I shared details with relatives and friends, many wanted to pitch in. They knew from me that the kids I met who battled cancer lived life with strength, courage, and smiles on their faces. They also had learned that pediatric cancer research is egregiously underfunded. Suddenly, our small bake sale was growing. We had many volunteer bakers, and before we knew it we had a local aquarium sign on as our location.

We used the Cookies for Kids' Cancer website to create a giving page in advance of our sale and let people know that no donation was too small. This was key. Before our actual bake sale, we had already raised thousands of dollars online. As for the sale itself, the day was incredibly special. Families and children made colorful signs to decorate our tables. The Glad Products Company was matching donations raised at that time, so when all was said and done, we raised over $30,000 total. It feels wonderful to know that something can be done in this fight. Children

need a voice, and we're thrilled that we can provide one for them through Cookies for Kids' Cancer.

Davidson, NC

DONNA REYNOLDS/MAGGIE THWAITES
Davidson, NC

Davidson, North Carolina, has supported Cookies for Kids' Cancer since it launched. Some events—like the Election Day Bake Sale—only come around once every 4 years, but two have become awesome annual traditions. Everyone here looks forward to the Christmas in Davidson Bake Sale and the Halloween Parade Bake Sale. Both take place on Main Street and bring out the best of what our town has to offer—cute kids, great bakers, and big hearts.

The Halloween sale is held at the end of the parade route, where children and dogs dress up in costumes to receive treats from local merchants. We set up our tent and inflatable snow globe in front of the post office, spotlight local kids fighting cancer on posters, and sell treats for all.

Christmas in Davidson coincides with our town's holiday festival. We have been in the same location for 5 years. The sale started with our Brownie Troop wanting to donate money to a children's charity. Since then, they have turned into socially aware teens who come together to run this sale as their school service project. This year, a group of four former Brownies ran the sale pretty much solo, baking, bagging, and selling cookies and taking turns working the booth. Prior to the big-deal parade when Santa rides in, some dedicated teen boys load baskets with baked goods and roam through town selling, returning with apron pockets bulging with cash.

Combined, these events have raised over $15,000 for pediatric cancer research. We can't wait to see what more small town bake sales can do to make a difference.

I am in awe every time we hold a bake sale at the generosity of the people of Davidson . . . I have never had an issue finding bakers, baggers, poster makers, and buyers.

Denny's

DENNY'S FAMILY RESTAURANTS
30 Locations in Western NY

From the very first holiday season of Cookies for Kids' Cancer, we've supported the cause by sending cookies to our Denny's team members who work on Christmas Day. It always felt like a special way to thank them for working so hard on a day most spend with their families. Then in 2011 when Liam Witt lost his battle with cancer, we decided it was time to bring our support for the organization directly to our dining guests at Denny's Family Restaurants.

In a few short weeks we organized a month-long promotion for 31 of our Upstate New York stores that invited our guests to "Be a Good Cookie" and donate to Cookies for Kids' Cancer at checkout. For each donation, the guest's name was placed on a paper cookie and used to decorate the walls.

Throughout the restaurant we had wonderful posters and

caddy toppers that told the story of Cookies and introduced our guests to Liam. The response from our guests and employees was off the charts. One guest emailed us after visiting one of our units and expressed, as a parent of a child who had battled cancer, how excited she was to learn about Cookies and know that a business in her community cared enough to support the fight against this terrible disease. It had us in tears, because that is the point: use our place in the community to connect, share, and give back in the most meaningful ways.

In 31 days, we introduced Cookies for Kids' Cancer to over 500,000 customers and raised over $75,000. We're excited to expand the promotion for a 2nd annual event to stores in Arizona during September to honor Pediatric Cancer Awareness Month.

LAURIE HEPPES/BEDWELL ELEMENTARY SCHOOL
Bernardsville, NJ

I teach kindergarten and I am in charge of community service at the Bedwell School in Bernardsville. I am always looking for a way for kids to help other kids. I heard about Cookies for Kids' Cancer over the summer and thought it would be a good thing for our kindergarten students to do, especially because there have been a few students at Bedwell who have gone through different cancer treatments. We thought it would be a great way for children to help other children in need.

In September, I along with the other kindergarten teachers decided to have a cookie sale. We asked our parents to bake with their children helping them. Then we had a sign up for selling; once again the parents had to do it with their children. The sale took place during our parent/teacher conferences so there would be a lot of adults in the building to purchase the cookies. The sale was a big hit and the children had a great time. They were so excited about helping other children. This was our first cookie sale, and we plan on doing it again next year with hopes that it will become a yearly event.

We had 12 students along with their parents selling the cookies and we had 47 bakers. All duties had to be done with their children. All of the cookies were sold by the dozen and packaged in a bag with a bow and a tag was connected to each bag that stated:

"Made with love by _____, Thank you for helping kids fight cancer."

We made $932 over 3 days.

index